THE
FRAGILITY
of CHINA

★

Breaking Points
of an Invincible Regime

By Dennis Unkovic

Encounter BOOKS

New York • London

First American edition published in 2024 by Encounter Books, an activity of Encounter for Culture and Education, Inc., a nonprofit, tax-exempt corporation. Encounter Books website address: www.encounterbooks.com

Manufactured in the United States and printed on acid-free paper. The paper used in this publication meets the minimum requirements of ANSI/NISO Z39.48-1992 (R 1997) (*Permanence of Paper*).

FIRST AMERICAN EDITION

LIBRARY OF CONGRESS CATALOGING-IN-PUBLICATION DATA IS AVAILABLE

Information for this title can be found at the Library of Congress website under the following ISBN 978-1-64177-391-1 and LCCN 2024007113.

DEDICATION

This book is dedicated to the men and women of the United States Armed Forces and Army Reserve who proudly and selflessly protect the interests of America around the world. Thank you for your service.

CONTENTS

SECTION III: WHAT THE WEST MUST DO

Contents

INTRODUCTION

More than twenty-five years ago, my family and I visited Aruba. One of the highlights of our trip was walking on the Natural Bridge located on Aruba's northeast coast. Naturally carved out of coral limestone by the Caribbean Sea over thousands of years, the formidable bridge spanned over 100 feet (30.43 meters) and rose 23 feet (7.01 meters) above the ocean. Standing on top of the bridge was thrilling as the waves crashed underneath. The bridge felt strong, powerful, and immortal. Then on September 2, 2005, the Natural Bridge suddenly collapsed into the Caribbean Sea. Despite its size and mighty appearance, the structure in reality was quite fragile.

Like the coral bridge giving the outward appearance of unwavering strength and endurance, today's China seems to be a force of nature. Prior to the 1960s, China was a desperately poor country with starving citizens and low potential. But decade by decade beginning in the 1980s, China evolved and grew and now boasts the second largest gross domestic product in the world (second only to the United States). It is possible that China's gross domestic product (GDP) will surpass that of the United States within the next two decades. Some observers go so far as to predict the 21st century will be the "Chinese Century." China's paramount leader, Xi Jinping, along with the Chinese Communist Party (CCP), is aggressively pressing forward with his grand vision of transforming China into the world's top economic and military power.

I have written this book because America and other Western countries need to understand exactly what is happening in China. For far too long, China has been viewed by the West as primarily an inexpensive manufacturing hub located at the center of the global supply chain. This is short-sighted and faulty thinking. China today represents a growing political force that left unchecked will exert massive worldwide influence over trade, international relations, and military might. More so than the USSR during the Cold War and Japan during its bubble period, China is formidable both economically and with its growing military potential. America's leaders need to make interacting with China the top national priority because China has the potential to displace the United States within the world economy. But is China's economic domination inevitable? For many reasons, no.

This book will examine what I call MaxTrends®. MaxTrends® are specific events or developments that can produce a measurable impact—positive or negative—on how nations, individuals, industries, and economies perform. MaxTrends® in a sense represent "breaking points" that demand some level of response or action in order to avoid short-term problems or long-term catastrophes. China may be in its ascendancy, but MaxTrends® have the potential to redirect, or in some cases prevent, Xi Jinping and the Chinese Communist Party from achieving their ambitious international agenda. How China recognizes and then addresses these MaxTrends® will ultimately determine the course of its future.

While I was a student at the University of Virginia, I became fascinated with China and Japan. Even back then, I recognized that both countries had great unrealized potential. As an international lawyer and speaker, I have visited China and Japan more than one hundred times. I developed my perspectives by helping U.S. companies establish manufacturing operations in China, transferring technologies, forming joint ventures between Chinese and Western companies, and advising Chinese entities on investing in the United States. I gained insights into how China overcame its Mao-era problems and became the unlikely success it did (simply put, the Chinese were more driven and focused than their competitors). After a career spent dealing with that part of the world, I recognize China's many assets and yet see the cracks in its foundation. Other authors may like to write to obtain favor with powerful Chinese interests. Instead, I try to frankly and honestly lay out China's strengths and weaknesses.

What readers will gain from this book is an understanding of China's existing strengths along with the many significant challenges Xi Jinping faces. The powerful and resilient facade that China projects to the world hides a fragility underneath. This book is about the structural fractures and outside pressures that could potentially lead to China's collapse.

SECTION I

APPEARANCE VERSUS REALITY

CHAPTER ONE

THE WORLD'S MOST POWERFUL MAN
Xi Jinping and His Three-Legged Stool

The year 2008 was truly a landmark for China and its leadership. Just four years earlier, the International Olympic Committee (IOC) had voted to accept Beijing's bid to host the 2008 Summer Olympic Games. Nearly everyone who attended the 2008 Summer Olympics and the millions who watched the events on television agreed that the Beijing Games were highly successful and served to greatly heighten China's global prestige. In a sense, the 2008 Summer Olympics were a coming-out party for China, which had gambled enormous financial and human resources in order to prove to the world that it was much more than just a massive manufacturing complex. By pulling off one of the most impressive Olympics in recent memory, China officially arrived on the world stage.

What few knew then, or perhaps even recognize now, is that an equally notable but far less public event was taking place behind the scenes. One individual from the Chinese Communist Party (CCP) was intimately involved in both the planning and execution of the 2008 Summer Olympics. That individual was Xi Jinping. For true insiders, though, it came as no surprise when an official announcement following the 2008 Olympics decreed that Xi Jinping would succeed China's then-leader Hu Jintao and assume China's top political position in 2013. This marked the beginning of Xi's transformation from a high-level CCP official into the undisputed leader of China.

Today Xi Jinping is the single most powerful leader in the world. His power rests on three bases: the CCP; China's economy; and the

Chinese military establishment. As the general secretary of the CCP, as the president of the People's Republic of China, and as chairman of the Central Military Commission, Xi has achieved complete control over all three sectors. No other world leader exerts such total control over a nation and its future. Xi is the strongest of the world's strong-men, and, as such, he can act faster and with greater impact than other world leaders. It is impossible to understand today's China without understanding Xi Jinping—who he is, where he came from, and how he plans to use his unprecedented power base to achieve his ambitious vision for China.

THE ROAD TO THE TOP IS NEVER A STRAIGHT LINE

Born in 1953, Xi's ultimate rise to power was neither preordained nor predictable. Had someone penned a novel describing Xi's journey to the top, few readers would see the story as realistic or believable. Nevertheless, Xi has managed to overcome numerous obstacles, some seemingly insurmountable, in reaching his current status as China's premier leader.

One of the darkest periods in China's long and turbulent history was the Cultural Revolution (1966–76). The Cultural Revolution was the nightmare creation of Mao Zedong, who ruled China from 1949 until his death in 1976. Following the devastating Great Chinese Fam-ine that ravaged China in the early 1960s, Mao imposed policies that completely upended Chinese society and its floundering economy. Mao's underlying goal during the Cultural Revolution was to ruthlessly excise all forms of "evil" capitalism from Chinese society. Mao's plan was pursued at all costs so as to guarantee that the Communist philosophy, which Mao promoted throughout his lifetime, would dominate China. In order to achieve his vision, all real or perceived political rivals of Mao were to be publicly identified and handled. Mao's infamous Red Guards traveled throughout the country, randomly attacking and exiling prominent individuals in government, academia, or industry who were viewed as threats to Mao's Communist principles. Many (including some of Mao's former fellow revolutionaries) were stripped of their titles and possessions and then exiled to the countryside or to factories as common laborers; some individuals simply disappeared. While Mao "officially" declared that the Cultural Revolution was ended in 1969, in reality the Red Guards continued to wreak havoc on China until Mao's death in 1976.

XI AND THE CULTURAL REVOLUTION

Prior to the Cultural Revolution, Xi Jinping's father, Xi Zhongxun, was a revered and highly ranked CCP veteran. Xi Zhongxun fought during the 1930s (pre–World War II) in Northwestern China alongside Mao and his cadre of loyal followers. Following the CCP's victory in 1949, Xi Zhongxun emerged as an important and well-respected figure within the hierarchy of the CCP. However, Xi's father fell from grace during the Cultural Revolution and was demoted from his position and reportedly jailed for some time.[1] Throughout this aberrant period, his teenage son—Xi Jinping—found himself exiled to a poor rural area of China and assigned to work on a farm for seven years. Xi has openly spoken of his experiences during those years. This would be a crucial turning point in Xi's life because he was forced to personally confront the devastating impact of Mao's Cultural Revolution on him and his family.

As a teenager, Xi decided his best way to move forward was to become a full-fledged member of the CCP. After he earned a degree in chemical engineering from the well-respected Beijing Tsinghua University, and after numerous attempts and rejections, Xi was eventually accepted as a CCP member. He was driven and competent and rapidly moved upward from one administrative role to another at various locations throughout China (at one point even spending some time with an American family in Iowa). After achieving success in a number of leadership positions, Xi was elected vice president of the People's Republic of China. That was a true turning point, because it was through this position that Xi came to plan and oversee the highly successful 2008 Summer Olympics in Beijing. Those games were Xi's springboard to the top. When the Olympics returned to Beijing for the 2022 Winter Games, Xi no longer lingered in the background. He proudly stood front and center at the Olympics as the most powerful political leader in the world.

THE THREE-LEGGED STOOL

While it may seem strange to describe Xi Jinping in those superlative terms, I believe it is accurate. My reasoning reflects my understanding of how China's power bases are structured and integrated. The best way to understand power in China is to picture a three-legged stool. A stool with only two legs is useless, but a stool with three sturdy legs, each equally important and dependent on the others, is totally stable. Think of China as a stool supported by three legs: (1) the powerful CCP; (2) the massive Chinese economy; and (3) China's rapidly growing military establishment.

In very short order, Xi gained control of all three legs of the stool. In 2012, he rose to become general secretary of the CCP. This party has only 98 million official members (2023 estimate). That relatively small number of individuals comprises the single political power bloc that exerts total control over the lives of 1.41 billion Chinese citizens. Xi, as the CCP general secretary, is at the top of the pyramid. There is no counterforce or apparent CCP opposition to him. Without question, whatever Xi decides or recommends to the Politburo or the periodic Party Congress becomes the way forward for China. Throughout this book, you will see numerous examples of the total control that Xi can and does exercise.

Xi's ascendency was preordained after the 2008 Olympics when it was announced to the world that Xi would succeed then-CCP-head Hu Jintao in four years. Xi procured the second leg also in 2012 when he was officially named chairman of the Central Military Commission, a position that guaranteed Xi's total control over the entire Chinese military. The third leg of the stool was secured in 2013, when Xi was elected president of the People's Republic of China. Being named president assured Xi absolute control over the Chinese government, its policies, and the then–rapidly expanding Chinese economy.

Once in place, Xi wasted no time in successfully consolidating his power within each of the three legs of the stool. The extent of his power became clear just four years later. Up until then, a CCP leader was expected to serve a maximum of ten years (two five-year terms) before being replaced by the next in line. Traditionally, at China's National People's Congress, after a leader has served an initial five-year term, a successor is named who officially takes over at the end of the leader's second five-year term. This is exactly what happened when Xi Jinping was designated as Hu Jintao's successor in 2008 and effectively took over in 2013. However, in 2018, the National People's Congress did not name a successor to Xi, as would be the normal procedure. Few outside observers doubt that Xi had somehow managed to convince the People's Congress to refrain from doing so.

Who is Xi Jinping, the person? I am not sure anyone can accurately answer that question. What is clear, though, from closely following his career and accomplishments, is that Xi is a complex individual with an extroverted personality. He works exceptionally hard at forging relationships with global leaders. His personality seems more nuanced than that of Kim Jong-un or Vladimir Putin. It is well known that Xi is an avid and passionate reader. Outlets throughout China promote lists of his favorite books. Now that Xi is in his third five-year term, he seems to favor embracing a cult of personality. This is unlike his immediate predecessors and more in the style of Mao.

The bottom line is that there is no other political leader of a major country today (except maybe for autocrats in a handful of nations) whose power is essentially unchallenged with no prospect of a successor in sight. This places Xi in the unique position of being solely able to dictate China's future path from economic, military, and political standpoints with basically no opposition. This is totally different from the United States. When an American president fails to receive congressional support on any decision or legislative agenda, the president is able to (and usually does) publicly pass the buck and blame the opposing political party for its intransigence and bad judgment. This is the famous Washington, DC, blame game, and it plays out regardless of which political party is in power. Xi does not face that situation in China. With effectively no opposing party or rivals, if Xi wants something, Xi can order it to be done.

Being unopposed, though, does come with one cost—there is no passing the buck in China. There is no one for Xi to blame if things go south, or at least there are no other credible scapegoats. He is vulnerable on many fronts since he controls everything. Xi alone is ultimately responsible for any and all of his decisions and the consequences, good or bad. China's mishandling of the COVID-19 crisis between 2020 and 2022 is a great example of a Xi-imposed policy that went awry. When Xi's "Zero-COVID" policy was abruptly reversed in December 2022, resulting in a greatly diminished Chinese economy, there was no one else to blame.

Many rock and roll fans, including myself, believe that the Rolling Stones are the greatest rock and roll group of all time. A highlight of every Stones concert is when the band blasts their 1969 classic "You Can't Always Get What You Want" and the crowds go wild. The fever pitch is still strong five decades later and shows no sign of slowing down anytime soon. In much the same way that the Rolling Stones continue holding on to their top spot in rock history, Xi Jinping, despite the many obstacles in his way, has managed to retain his sole leadership of China with no end in sight.

This book will look at the goals of today's China as espoused under Xi Jinping's leadership. While rarely transparent, Xi has increasingly made it clear that his ultimate goal is for China to dominate the world economically and militarily. As we'll see, thirteen MaxTrends® stand in the way of this goal. First, though, we need to understand something about China's history and how it has bred a deep distrust of the West.

CHAPTER TWO

WHY CHINA DISTRUSTS THE WEST
The Dark Ages

*China deeply distrusts the West and believes Western powers are once
again trying to suppress China's global ambitions. When you look back
over the last 500 years, the Chinese have reasons to harbor this belief.
China has a long and tumultuous history with the West, and the only
way to truly understand today's China and the agenda of its leader, Xi
Jinping, is to understand its past.*

CHINA 1500 BCE TO 1423 CE

When the ancient Egyptian civilization reached its peak more
than 3,500 years ago, most of today's Europe was a wild, unex-
plored place. The tribes inhabiting it were mostly hunter-gatherers
struggling to survive. Yet, five thousand miles to the east, another
civilization was flourishing with its own unique language and an
advanced culture that was responsible for many world-changing
achievements. Physically and psychologically isolated from the West,
China was known as the Middle Kingdom. The period that most
scholars and historians rank as the true golden age of Chinese civilization was the Tang Dynasty between 618 CE and 907 CE (except
for a brief interregnum between 690 CE and 705 CE). Chinese arts
and culture during the Tang Dynasty were simply extraordinary. One
ruler, Taizong, was responsible for significant innovations in China's
educational system, governmental structures, religious practices, and
social networks. Some of Emperor Taizong's contributions are still

evident in China today. Perhaps the most world-changing invention during Taizong's reign was the woodblock printing press. This extraordinary innovation enabled the Chinese to capture, retain, and efficiently disseminate information throughout the land.

China's Song Dynasty (also known as the Sung Dynasty) from 960 CE to 1279 CE was an unsettled period in China's history as the country experienced bitter political infighting and the rise of conservatism. Events reversed course during the Yuan Dynasty (1271 CE to 1368 CE), when the Mongols invaded from the north and wrested control over China. Around this time, the famed Venetian explorer Marco Polo made his long journey over the Silk Road from Italy to China. Polo's vivid descriptions of what he encountered in the Far East and China ignited intense interest throughout Europe.

CHINA'S FIVE CENTURIES OF DARKNESS

During the Ming Dynasty (1368 CE to 1644 CE), China successfully managed to retain the integrity of its borders while at the same time seeking to extend its influence around the world. This led to a truly crucial event in China's history. Around 1423 CE, China's global outreach abruptly came to an end. (For fascinating insights into this period, read *1421: The Year China Discovered America* by Gavin Menzies.)

Under the third emperor of the Ming Dynasty, Zhu Di, China's seagoing fleet was vastly expanded and reportedly consisted of more than 681 ships. Emperor Zhu, even more than his predecessors, was passionately committed to expanding China's influence and reach around the world. Believing that exploring and controlling the oceans was the only way to accomplish this, Zhu ordered the construction of a massive Chinese fleet. These ships were divided into three separate fleets and set sail in 1421, with each fleet traveling in a different direction for the next three years. Menzies theorizes that the fleet under the leadership of Admiral Zheng actually reached North America in 1422.

In Menzies's *1421*, he offers up varying degrees of proof about what happened during these years, such as ballast stones found in California that could only have come from China. However, what we do know is that in late 1423, the three fleets returned to China, all somewhat diminished in size from when they left. Upon the fleets' return, Emperor Zhu was critically ill, and China found itself in the midst of widespread economic and military turmoil. Then, Emperor Zhu died, and—to the bewilderment of historians—his son, Zhu Gaosui, ordered the destruction of all remaining ships in that vast Chinese fleet. In a single stroke, Zhu Gaosui reversed China's expansion and effectively brought its outward-looking ambitions to a full stop. Because of Zhu Gaosui's actions, China turned inward both physically and psychologically for the next five hundred years. Thus began a dark period in Chinese history that China today would rather forget.

EUROPE EXPLOITS CHINA

Beginning around 1424, China became an extraordinarily inward-looking nation that permitted only limited contact with the outside world. Recognizing this, seafaring countries throughout Europe saw an opening and began taking advantage of China's self-imposed vulnerability. The burgeoning European merchant class came to covet the vast wealth and resources that China possessed—no matter the cost.[2]

Over the next five hundred years, until the early 20th century, European nations (most notably Britain) ruthlessly exploited China and its economy. European trading companies with the backing of naval armadas sought out commerce and opportunities not just in China but throughout much of Southeast Asia. One of the largest (and most infamous) trading companies of the day was the East India Company. The East India Company gutted China and much of Asia by unceasingly extracting riches bound for Europe. The most shameful chapter of this company's run was its strategy to smuggle opium into China, encouraging addiction among the Chinese in order to gain economic advantages. Since Europe had an extraordinary appetite for Chinese teas, one way to guarantee easy access to China's tea crops was to weaken the will of the Chinese people by selling them opium. Sadly, the strategy worked. When the Chinese government finally stepped in, the First Opium War between China and Britain broke out. The war did not last long, and the Chinese were badly defeated by Britain's superior naval forces. Using its victory in the Opium War as an excuse, Britain forced China to enter into a 150-year lease of what is today's Hong Kong SAR (Special Administrative Region).

At the height of the West's efforts to formally colonize China, the Treaty of Nanking (1842) was used to impose trading rights over the Chinese in what is today's Shanghai along the Huangpu River. The British and the Americans (as well as the French, Germans, and others) created the international settlement in Shanghai known as the Bund. Trading companies that for centuries had been ransacking China achieved their strongest foothold along the Bund at the end of the 19th century. This and the events that preceded it have always been a national embarrassment for the Chinese and set the stage for China's rejection of the West during the 20th century. China's five hundred years of domination by Western powers were about to come to an end.

CHINA POST-1949

In 1949, the Chinese Communist Party under the leadership of Mao Zedong finally gained control over the "People's Republic of China." Following Mao's death in 1976, China rapidly expanded its economic status under three generations of CCP leadership until Xi Jinping formally assumed power in 2013. As the single most powerful world leader since World War II, Xi views China as a dominant global economic and military power that will never again kowtow to the West.

Given this history, any investor, company, or foreign government expecting to successfully conduct business with China is destined to fail unless they first understand the scars in China's psyche. Western perspectives on modern China are shaped by China's xenophobia, Communist system, and sometimes brutal repression of dissent, but this doesn't tell the whole story. Xi Jinping's grand visions for China's future are in part a response to this difficult past. But no path is a straight line, and Xi faces major obstacles in his efforts. This book will examine these obstacles—which I call MaxTrends®—and predict whether Xi Jinping will or will not ultimately succeed.

CHAPTER THREE

MAXTRENDS®
(or, What Keeps Xi Jinping Awake at Night)

*One of America's premier art forms is musical theater, which brings
memorable and moving stories to life through words, dance, and song.
Who can't recall a song or character from* Oklahoma, West Side Story,
A Chorus Line, Phantom of the Opera, Wicked, *or* The Lion King?
In 2015, the smash Broadway musical Hamilton *changed the game for
stage productions to follow. Weaving together a soundtrack of hip-hop,
R&B, and traditional showtunes with a fascinating true story, creator
Lin-Manuel Miranda manages in a few hours to teach audiences
more about America's revolutionary history and the life of Alexander
Hamilton than they likely ever learned in school. One enigmatic
historical figure depicted in* Hamilton *is King George III, who, except
for Queen Elizabeth II's seventy years on the throne, was the longest-
serving monarch in British history. King George III began his reign
during the period just prior to the American Revolution, as Britain was
near an apex of its global power and influence. Britain's navy controlled
the seas and protected the valuable trade routes backed by British
armies garrisoned all over the world.*

In a sense, King George III resembles China's current leadership.
Aside from an opportunistic Parliament, George III's powers as ruling
monarch went largely unchallenged. Whatever George wanted, he got.
Likewise, effectively no political counterweight exists to Xi Jinping's
power and his dreams of transforming China into the world's leading
economic power and military behemoth. In China's autocratic society,
Xi sits in the ultimate position, which, in theory, means that whatever
policy Xi desires will be implemented without challenge. With no successor in the wings, nothing seems to stand in his way.

Because Xi and the leadership of the Chinese Communist Party have no real opposition, they probably assume the success of their plans is preordained. It is not. Despite his unique power base, Xi Jinping faces real obstacles—breaking points—that have the potential to divert or block his ambitions of transforming China into a global leader. This book presents what I believe are Xi's thirteen most serious challenges—I call them MaxTrends®.[1]

WHAT ARE MAXTRENDS®?

MaxTrends® is the word I use in this book to identify a development or event that has the potential to impact a country and its leaders in such a way as to affect their ability to transform their policies into reality. MaxTrends® differ from what we usually think of as "trends." Trends are TikTok challenges, mocktails, or shopping local. MaxTrends® are overarching external factors that, if not properly managed, can alter the direction in which a country is headed. Far too often, MaxTrends® and their effects are not recognized, taken seriously, or adequately dealt with by global leaders. Examples of MaxTrends® include pollution, global warming, endemic corruption, dysfunctional supply chains, demographic shifts, threats of cyber warfare, evolving social policies, political hot spots, new technologies, and more. This book focuses on MaxTrends® that have the potential to change the course that China is on.

THE IMPACT OF MAXTRENDS® ON XI JINPING

There are thirteen key MaxTrends® that pose significant challenges to the goals of China's current leadership and have the greatest potential to alter the path that Xi Jinping has so carefully laid out for China since he came to power in 2013. Some MaxTrends® could fundamentally disrupt China's economy, which prior to the last half decade grew explosively since the 1980s. Other MaxTrends® reflect how the CCP under Xi Jinping's leadership has abandoned the successful and less intrusive policies of Xi's predecessors who came to power following the death of Mao Zedong in 1976. Xi has very different and more expansionistic ambitions for China.

Under Xi Jinping, China is imposing unparalleled levels of control over its economy, private industry, and the lives of the Chinese people. Examples include Xi's ongoing anticorruption campaign directed at both government officials and commercial entities, the role played by China's currency (the renminbi), and China's open disregard for the essential role intellectual property plays in fostering new technologies and innovation. How China responds to the following MaxTrends® will be pivotal in how China will fare throughout the balance of the 21st century.

13 MAXTRENDS® THAT WILL BEDEVIL XI JINPING

MaxTrend® #1: Too Few People

The demographic tides are inexorably flowing against China. China's ill-conceived one-child policy is an example of a policy gone terribly wrong. China faces a rapidly aging population as a result of its plummeting birth rate, and this could derail Xi Jinping's ambitious plans for China's future.

MaxTrend® #2: Taiwan

Taiwan was and remains a major irritant for Xi Jinping and the CCP. While it poses no military threat, Taiwan clearly frustrates Xi, who seems obsessed with pressuring Taiwan to abandon its democratic form of government and be folded into the People's Republic of China. While this may be what Xi and China ultimately want, an overt invasion or boycott of Taiwan by China would create an unprecedented crisis resulting in China alienating nations in the Southeast Asia region and around the world.

MAXTREND® #3: GLOBAL COMPETITION FOR RARE EARTH ELEMENTS

Rare earth elements (REEs) play a critical role in AI, quantum computing, and other key technologies. China today finds itself in a unique position to leverage its capability to both mine and refine REEs. However, countries around the world are seriously exploring ways to source their needed REEs domestically or in regions other than China. How this plays out in the long run will impact whether China can retain its lead and influence in sourcing REEs.

MAXTREND® #4: THE ONE-TWO PUNCH OF BAD REAL ESTATE AND MANIPULATED CURRENCY

China is trying to become a global leader, not just as an exporter of products, but also by effectively expanding the impact of its currency. Two things stand in the way. The first is China's failing real estate market and the resulting impact on China's economy. The second is that China's renminbi (RMB) remains an outlier currency. Both of these problems represent serious economic barriers to a globally ambitious China.

MAXTREND® #5: A FRACTURED GLOBAL SUPPLY CHAIN

For thirty years, China through careful planning (and a bit of luck) was able to construct a highly effective and efficient supply chain supported by a world-class infrastructure. This accelerated over three decades of economic growth and was even more powerful when combined with China's highly skilled yet (at the time) low-cost labor. Without question, the global supply chain was already exhibiting signs of breakage before 2020; however, the fracturing markedly increased during COVID-19 and does not promise to improve anytime soon. This will seriously depress China's future growth prospects.

MAXTREND® #6: WORSENING CLIMATE CHANGE AND POLLUTING POLICIES

At this point, no one can deny that serious global climate change is occurring. As the world's largest emitter of CO_2 gases, China has failed to take aggressive action to lessen its harmful impact on the planet, taking a toll on both China's people and global reputation.

MaxTrend® #7: Toxic Air and Not Enough Water

Toxic air and lack of potable water throughout China are a true and constant threat. Air and water pollution directly affect the health of the Chinese people and will, if not dealt with soon, create a basis for political instability—something that Xi Jinping must avoid at all costs.

MaxTrend® #8: The Corrosive Effects of Corruption

Corruption in China is an ongoing challenge for Xi Jinping and the CCP. To be fair, China is not alone. Corruption exists everywhere. However, the massive amount of power concentrated in Xi and particularly the CCP's 98 million members, if not properly controlled, will damage China's ability to reach its goals.

MaxTrend® #9: The Global Arms Race

Even prior to Xi Jinping, China was rapidly building up its military capabilities. This accelerated under Xi, so China now has a truly impressive military with both offensive and defensive capabilities. This is ironic because China has no serious or direct threats to its sovereignty in Asia or elsewhere. What China has done by its military expenditures is exacerbate an already rapidly growing global arms race. Situating military bases throughout the South China Sea, combined with its obsession with Taiwan, only serves to diminish China's role as a global leader and further creates a wedge between China and its trading partners in Asia and Australia.

MaxTrend® #10: The Rise of Nationalism

Something few expected as the world moved into the 21st century was that the "nation-state" mentality (which directly led to the atrocities of World War II) would return with such a vengeance. This challenges China and other countries when trying to impose their policies on other nations they hope to influence or make close allies. One reaction has been the increase of barriers to inbound and outbound foreign investment, which promises to decelerate China's expansive and costly Belt and Road Initiative.

MAXTREND® #11: STRUGGLING FOR TECH/INNOVATION DOMINANCE

Xi Jinping and Chinese regulators have imposed restraints on Chinese tech companies while at the same time insisting that tech leaders expand China's technology base and global reach. Xi dreams of establishing a two-technology world—one composed of Western-based technologies and one dominated by the Chinese. He can't have it both ways. Forcing overly restrictive limitations on tech companies and entrepreneurs of all sizes is bound to stifle China's quest for innovation and new technologies.

MAXTREND® #12: REJECTING FOREIGN INVESTMENT

After three decades of aggressively encouraging all kinds of foreign investment in China, Xi Jinping has reversed course. While companies around the world were at first slow to react, Xi's new policy is seriously hampering the flow of capital and technologies destined for China.

MAXTREND® #13: CONTROLLING INTELLECTUAL PROPERTY

Like other Asian nations, China for decades has had weak laws protecting intellectual property and only selectively enforced those laws when it was in its best interest. As larger Chinese companies now attempt to expand into global markets, the importance to them of protecting intellectual property is much different than it was in the past. It is not clear whether China understands (or cares) how its stance on intellectual property hurts its reputation in international markets.

In 2049, China will celebrate the one hundredth anniversary of the Chinese Revolution, which is when Mao Zedong and his supporters finally succeeded in gaining complete control over China and its political system. Perhaps the single overriding goal of the CCP under Xi Jinping is to guarantee China's position as the world's top economic center and military power before this anniversary occurs. This is a driving force behind China's highly ambitious and costly Belt and Road Initiative.[2] The Chinese government has already committed trillions of dollars to opening land and sea trade routes between Europe and China. This is not simply a question of money; the Belt and Road Initiative requires the agreement and involvement of many different countries. And to further complicate things for China, the MaxTrends® described in this book will pose daunting and ongoing challenges to this endeavor.

Even England's King George III during his unchallenged leadership had worries that kept him awake at night. Despite all of his royal power and command, the American Revolution succeeded. Xi and his colleagues should take note. Whether China truly recognizes its challenges and deals with them effectively will determine its future course.

SECTION II

MAXTRENDS®

CHAPTER FOUR

TOO FEW PEOPLE
China's Demographic Black Hole

Of all the MaxTrends® impacting Xi Jinping and China, perhaps the most significant and potentially devastating can be summarized in just two words—population decline. How can this be? According to the United Nations, China's population in 2023 was approximately 1.41 billion. Demographics, though, are like the tides—they never stop relentlessly shifting and shaping the future of humanity. What the size of China's population does not reveal is that China's fertility rate in 2022 dropped to nonsustainable levels while the number of Chinese citizens over the age of sixty is rising. Going forward, China's declining population will have an enormous impact on Xi Jinping and his lofty ambitions.

If you visit China, be it Shanghai, Ningbo, Wuhan, Harbin, or Beijing, take a few minutes and walk down any street. Don't look at the storefronts or buildings; look at the people. You will see many couples, but very few of those couples will have a child. Certainly don't expect to see a couple with two (or more) children. Sightings of families with young children are rare—and the clearest sign of a demographic breakdown already underway.

Like all savvy political leaders, Xi Jinping fully understands the key role a strong and productive workforce plays in determining China's future as a global power. Any country desiring to ensure its long-term economic growth and, most importantly, political stability must have a sufficient supply of capable workers. Unfortunately for Xi and the CCP, they are now facing a critical challenge that could derail their ambitious goals as they look forward to the CCP's one hundredth anniversary in 2049. Simply put, China's population is declining because too few children are being born to replace the retiring and aging workforce.

How did China arrive at this point? Perhaps part of the blame can be placed on the 18th-century economist Thomas Robert Malthus. Born in England in 1766, Malthus earned his reputation as a demographer.[1] Prior to the rise of the Industrial Revolution in mid-19th-century Europe and America, Malthus and his colleagues were intrigued by the global population trends they identified and their expected impact on the future availability of food supplies. Malthus predicted that while populations tended to grow exponentially, humankind's ability to produce enough food for the populace would only increase arithmetically. This led Malthus to ominously warn that over time the global population would explode, resulting in massive food shortages over large portions of the earth. No surprise, in his *Essay on the Principle of Population* (1798), Malthus cautioned that the world would find itself in a catastrophic state of starvation at some future point, and this triggered genuine alarm among governments and politicians. No one knows for sure whether the Qing Dynasty emperors were influenced by Malthus and his writings, but since his ideas were so widespread and commented upon throughout the 19th century, it is inconceivable that they did not reach the ears of Chinese officials.

In his writings, Malthus did acknowledge that significant events such as wars, famines, poor working/living conditions, and health pandemics could act to slow population growth. Nevertheless, Malthus predicted that an overpopulated and underfed world was inevitable. In the 19th century when Malthus was expounding his theories, the global population was about 1.5 billion. Roughly 160 years later, in 1959, the global population was 2.98 billion, and today the world counts over 8 billion people (with China accounting for about 18 percent of the total population).

Chinese leaders are clearly worried about their country's predicted inevitable population decline. Even Xi Jinping has publicly spoken on the impact of China's falling birth rate on its economy. In late October 2023, Xinhua—China's official government-sponsored news agency—revealed Xi's decree that Chinese women need to recognize a "new trend of family." Addressing a meeting of the All China Women's Federation, Xi reportedly said that Chinese women must "actively cultivate a new culture of marriage and childbearing and strengthen guidance on young people's view on marriage, childbirth and family." In other words, Xi is urging woman of a certain age to have more children, even if this means leaving the workforce. Whether his decree is taken seriously, only time will tell.

In another sign of apparent desperation, China has implemented what is known as the "double reduction" strategy. This initiative targets Chinese couples, particularly those in the upper middle class, who have one child. It is not unusual for couples in this demographic to spend up to 50 percent of their discretionary income on after-school tutoring in subjects such as math, science, foreign language, and music in order to give their child a head start in China's highly competitive adult society. However, Chinese leaders believe too much focus on one child will have a negative effect on society and want to "encourage" larger families. The Chinese government has gone so far as to back up this double-reduction initiative with the imposition of fines and even possible imprisonment for not having more children. So far this has resulted in the market for private tutors and music teachers drying up, and, interestingly, piano manufacturers in China have experienced double-digit declines in sales. And yet, China's birth rate remains unchanged.

HOW DID CHINA GET HERE?

I use the 1959 population statistic for a specific reason. 1959 was a critical year for China. Between 1959 and 1961, China suffered what is known as the Great Chinese Famine. This was a horrific period in

China's history as millions of its people died of starvation. With the benefit of hindsight, one can see that multiple factors were responsible for the famine, but two stand out from the others: (1) natural disasters (droughts, floods); and (2) the impact of the failed Great Leap Forward policy imposed on the Chinese populace by then-leader Mao Zedong. Eventually China overcame this tragic period, and slowly the population began to recover and grow. However, as China distanced itself from the disastrous social policies pursued by Mao, CCP leaders who had followed him feared that a spiking population would negate their new policies that were intended to grow China's economy and secure its future.

To counter what they considered a serious threat, in 1979 CCP leaders proposed and adopted a one-child policy that was rigorously enforced throughout China. The theory was that by significantly suppressing population growth through limiting the number of children born, China could more swiftly lift itself out of poverty (mirroring the theories of Malthus). Because the power that the Chinese government was able to exert over its citizens was so absolute, for the next three decades the one-child policy was far more effective than even the most optimistic Chinese leaders had predicted. One unanticipated and harmful consequence was the creation of a significant gender imbalance between Chinese males and females of a certain age (due to the fact that male babies in a Confucian Chinese society have been historically favored). While the statistics are not precise, the ratio in China today in a certain age sector is roughly 105.7 million males for every 100 million females. While this ratio has decreased somewhat from its peak in 2004, it continues to pose significant social implications for Chinese society.

In addition to harmful societal issues generated by the gender imbalance, China's one-child policy also resulted in a Chinese workforce that is rapidly aging, with fewer children being born to replenish it. China faces the daunting prospect of an insufficient number of workers over the next half century. It may seem hard to believe that China, with a population of about 1.41 billion, is suffering a labor shortage, but it is. And as more Chinese workers reach retirement age, there are increasing demands on Chinese society to support those aging individuals. Unlike the United States, China lacks a workable social security net for retirees, so the responsibility of caring for the elderly inevitably falls on family members. The situation is exacerbated by the cultural Chinese view on retirement age. Today, most Chinese optimistically plan to retire, if possible, by age fifty-four. There are laws in China providing that sixty is the age when men are "expected"—or required—to retire. For women, the retirement age is fifty-five, and women who are considered "blue collar" workers can reasonably expect to retire at age fifty. The National People's Congress in 2021 recognized the potentially dire economic implications of this and recommended that China's legal retirement ages be raised as a way to slow the rapidly shrinking labor pool. To put China's challenge into real terms, by 2035 China will have about four hundred million people who are at least sixty years old and no longer working. This will amount to over 30 percent of the population.

It is an established fact that any society needs 2.1 births per female to maintain a certain level of population stability. Otherwise, populations will inevitably decline (this is referred to as a "baby bust"). However, birth trends are moving in the opposite direction, and China is not alone. For example, South Korea's total fertility rate (TFR) is 1.11, which is 50 percent less than the necessary replacement rate of 2.1. When too few children are born, labor shortages result and eventually pension-fund crises are unavoidable because of insufficient funds to support those who are no longer working. The only possible solution is government-sanctioned immigration, which is not popular in most homogenous Asian societies, including China.

An equally apt example of a nation facing critical population decline is Japan. While Japan experienced significant economic growth during the 1960s (at times as high as 10 percent), its population began to markedly decline around twenty years ago. As a result, Japan's national economic growth rate has remained suppressed. When China's leadership recognized this disturbing trend in Japan, its answer was to revise China's one-child policy that had been in place for decades. In 2015, to the surprise of many, China's leadership publicly declared that married couples would now be "allowed" (and even encouraged) to have two children. This policy reversal was an obvious attempt to revive the rapidly aging Chinese labor force. The double whammy of a declining birth rate combined with a longer life expectancy for the average Chinese citizen was a critical challenge the Chinese leadership hoped to surmount. But there was little positive public acceptance, and still not enough babies were being born.

How far things had gone became crystal clear in 2020. Every ten years, China conducts its nationwide census, and the 2020 census contained some fascinating data. Perhaps the most striking was how the working-age population in China is drastically declining. For example, during the prior census in 2011, China's working-age population came to 70 percent. By 2020, that had shrunk to 63.3 percent—quite an amazing decline in just a decade. Even worse, over the next five years, China's workforce is expected to shrink by 35 million workers. In 2021, the CCP's top policy body, the Politburo, declared that married Chinese couples were now allowed (and, again, encouraged) to have *three* children. Why? Because the two-child policy initiated five years earlier had not reversed China's declining birth rate. In fact, in 2020, there were just 12 million births, the lowest number recorded in China since 1961. Still, there was no positive response.

The inescapable challenge facing Xi Jinping and China's leadership today is how to regenerate a country that for nearly forty years followed a strict policy of deliberately suppressing population growth. And it is not just a function of "permission" to have children—an equally critical factor is the extremely high cost of raising a family in China. Many married couples in China who have managed to achieve a certain level of financial security have simply elected not to have children at all.

It is striking to see how rapidly birth trends have reversed in really a short amount of time. In the 1960s, when China was largely an agriculturally based economy, the typical Chinese family had on average six children. By the 1980s, when the one-child policy came into effect, the average Chinese family had shrunk to three children.[2] And today, as evidenced on the city sidewalks, the typical Chinese family has two, one, or perhaps no children at all. This poses serious problems for Xi Jinping and the CCP because of the major staffing problems being felt throughout many Chinese industries. It will only get worse going forward. A labor shortage of even greater magnitude than the one China is currently experiencing promises to cripple Chinese productivity, which has been a critical factor in China's growth over the last three decades. For Xi, there is no obvious short- or long-term solution to this most basic but disturbing MaxTrend®.

CHAPTER FIVE

TAIWAN
The Thorn in China's Side

Taiwan is the itch that China dares not scratch. As much as Xi Jinping desires to impose a reunification strategy with Taiwan, the consequences of doing so by military force would ignite massive negative political and economic responses from nations worldwide. Russia's unprovoked invasion of Ukraine in 2022 and the subsequent economic sanctions imposed on Russia and its elites should serve as a warning to China. Nonetheless, China is obsessed with reuniting Taiwan and China and continues to pursue military actions that reinforce this obsession—flying sorties daily over Taiwan, venturing into Taiwan's sovereign waters— all as part of its Grey Zone strategy. This chapter examines the only three options China has: (1) invading Taiwan's outlying islands; (2) quarantining Taiwan; or (3) pursuing a full-on military invasion—and why none of these will result in a good outcome for China.

Taiwan (the Republic of China or ROC) is an island just off the coast of China with about 23.9 million inhabitants. While the country was at first ruled by an autocratic government, Taiwan transformed itself into a vibrant democracy after 1949. Despite its small geographic footprint, Taiwan boasts a strong and highly productive economy and serves as headquarters for some of the world's most successful corporations, many possessing leading-edge technologies. Taiwan dominates the silicon chip manufacturing industry and is home to the Taiwan Semiconductor Manufacturing Company Limited (TSMC), the global leader in producing the most advanced and smallest microprocessors.

While Taiwan poses absolutely no military or economic threat to the People's Republic of China, China is obsessed with Taiwan. One reason is that, aside from the physical borders of this island nation, Taiwan has claimed jurisdiction over Taiping Island in the South China Sea as well as other archipelagos (Penghu, Matsu, Kinmen, Pratas) located throughout the South and East China Seas. The major threat Taiwan faces is posed by the increasingly aggressive military maneuvers and political strategies pursued by China that are intended to undercut Taiwan's sovereignty.

Why China is so obsessed with the reunification of Taiwan and the Mainland is not an enigma. It is based on national pride, which is the core of Xi Jinping's leadership philosophy. China tries to justify its claims to sovereignty over Taiwan based on Taiwan's history. After Taiwan was first colonized by the Dutch, who ruled between 1624 and 1668, the emperors of China's Qing Dynasty ruled Taiwan beginning in 1688 until the time of the Sino–Japanese War (1894–1895), when the Chinese were soundly defeated by the Japanese. The outcome was Taiwan becoming a Japanese colony, which continued until Japan's unconditional surrender at the end of World War II. This finally fully untethered Taiwan from Japan.

In 1945, the Kuomintang Party led by Chiang Kai-shek continued its confrontation with the Mao Zedong–led Chinese Communist Party, each jockeying for control of Mainland China. Chiang Kai-shek lost the fight four years later. At that point, he and his followers fled to Taiwan, which they named the Republic of China. Shortly afterward, the United States established a mutual defense treaty with Taiwan. That close relationship continued until former president Richard Nixon unexpectedly declared a major shift in traditional U.S. foreign policy. In a bold move, Nixon opened up America's relations with Mainland China and the leaders of the CCP just three years before Mao died. This resulted in a number of "communiqués," first issued under President Nixon and later continued under the Carter Administration. In essence, the communiqués declared that as far as the United States was concerned, there was "One China and Taiwan is part of China." This in short became known as the One China policy. Nevertheless, the Carter Administration between 1977 and 1980 still maintained unofficial relations with the people of Taiwan and ROC government officials.

THE U.S. CONGRESS AND THE ONE CHINA POLICY

Interestingly, the U.S. Congress felt more strongly than the Carter Administration about supporting Taiwan, and so the Taiwan Relations Act (TRA) was passed by Congress and signed into law in 1979. The TRA does not "officially" recognize the Republic of China; it instead refers to "governing authorities of Taiwan." The TRA stated that it was formal U.S. policy to "consider any effort to determine the future of Taiwan by other than peaceful means, including by boycotts or embargoes, a threat to the peace and security of the Western Pacific area, and of grave concern to the United States." This strong diplomatic language was intended as a proverbial stick in the eye to China's sovereignty claims over Taiwan and served as the justification for America to continue selling advanced defensive military equipment to Taiwan. The Reagan, Clinton, and George W. Bush Administrations from time to time offered veiled commentaries on the One China policy, but did not back away from its language.

Even during the Obama Administration, the United States continued the status quo by selling defensive weapons to Taiwan. Then, in a move that surprised many observers, the Trump Administration raised the U.S. government's support for Taiwan to an even higher level. When the Biden Administration took over in 2021, it refused to reverse Trump's policy and continued to aid Taiwan while political and economic tensions increased between America and China. Basically, the U.S. policy toward Taiwan is and has to be intentionally ambiguous. Whether the U.S. government would go to war with China if Taiwan were attacked by the People's Republic remains an open question.

XI JINPING AND TAIWAN

This brings us to Xi Jinping. Xi has adopted a far more aggressive stance than his predecessors in pursuing both military and economic strategies designed to assert China's dominion over Taiwan. Since coming to power in 2013, Xi has devoted vast financial resources to strengthening China's military and naval capacities, and this directly impacts Taiwan. Why the military buildup? Because Xi knows that any planned invasion or attack on Taiwan would pose significant logistical challenges for the Chinese. Unlike Russia invading Ukraine in 2022, China cannot directly deploy tanks and other land-based military equipment because Taiwan is an island that is well defended.

Aware of these logistical challenges, China has increasingly engaged in a form of targeted harassment often referred to as "Grey Zone conflict." This includes flying sorties of Chinese military aircraft into Taiwan's airspace at irregular intervals, thus forcing the Taiwanese air force to send up its own fighter aircraft in response. This same game is played when Chinese military ships venture into Taiwan's sovereign waters without permission. Pursuing Grey Zone activities provides two advantages for the Chinese. First, how Taiwan's military responds educates Chinese military leaders about the level of sophistication of Taiwan's armed forces. Second, having to repel every unauthorized incursion becomes a very expensive task for Taiwan's military. China continues to publicly proclaim to the world that it is unhappy with the current relationship and wants to absorb Taiwan into the PRC. However, Taiwan refuses to abandon its democracy and prefers to trumpet its positive relationship with the United States over a closer relationship with China.

CHINA'S THREE OPTIONS

With Xi Jinping and China's leadership dead set on reunification with Taiwan, China has basically three options to consider. The first option for China is to invade the outlying islands claimed by Taiwan that are located in the East and South China Seas. Possible targets would include Taiping Island, which is located near the Spratly group of islands in the South China Sea, Pratas Island near the Philippines, and the Penghu Islands near Southern Taiwan. The Penghu Islands are, in fact, very close to Mainland China, as are the Kinmen and Matsu Islands, which are also claimed by Taiwan. Because China currently has the largest navy in the world (as measured solely by number of ships), the Chinese navy already possesses the ability to seize control over some or all of these islands from Taiwan. But is this a smart thing for China to do? While China currently has the capability to overrun and gain physical control of the outlying islands, this would not directly impact Taiwan itself. Plus, China would be forced to deal with immediate negative reactions from the United States, Japan, Korea, the Philippines, and other nations, particularly those in the Asian region. Nations throughout Asia would clearly consider China's unprovoked invasion of these islands a direct threat to their own borders and sovereignty. This would in turn trigger the likelihood of punitive trade restrictions or prohibitions on the ability of Chinese companies to export products around the world. In short, other than allowing the country to scratch a persistent itch, invading these islands would create no long-term benefits for China.

A second option would require carefully coordinated steps by the Chinese military to establish a "quarantine" of Taiwan's waters and the airspace surrounding Taiwan and its possessions. While possible, this would be a massive and expensive undertaking by the Chinese air force and navy. I expect Chinese leaders would try to justify a quarantine as a way for China to block the importation of military equipment that might be supplied to Taiwan by the United States and other countries. Again, the risk for China under this scenario would be the certain rapid and unfavorable international responses, though perhaps slightly less severe than in the case of invading the islands off the coast of Taiwan. Without a doubt, this would force the United States to consider setting up its own counterblockade of ships going into China. That prospect would directly disrupt the global supply chain and China's role in it, but ultimately do great harm to the world economy.

The third, and most extreme, option for China is to carry out a full military invasion of Taiwan. This would at first involve China's navy and air force, but eventually all Chinese armed forces would be engaged. This option certainly would be the most expensive and politically risk-laden effort on China's part. Any invasion scenario is fraught with countless risks and would clearly be viewed by Japan as a direct threat to its national sovereignty. While up until this point Japan has refused to develop its own nuclear weapons, in my view this could definitely change following an unprovoked invasion of Taiwan by China. Few experts doubt that Japan within a very short period of time could develop its own nuclear capabilities, as this would send a clear signal to discourage the Chinese from targeting Japan next. Of course, there is the very real prospect that an unprovoked invasion of Taiwan by China could trigger a larger war if the United States came to the defense of Taiwan by either supplying it with military equipment or directly engaging American troops.

Since there is no positive benefit likely from any of the three options, why Xi Jinping feels that reunification with Taiwan is such a high national priority is something understood only by Xi and the CCP leadership. One wild card for Xi to consider is whether the United States would come to the aid of Taiwan if it were to be attacked or embargoed by China. The U.S. has maintained a deliberately opaque policy as to how it would respond in such circumstances.

NANCY PELOSI VISITS TAIWAN

From time to time over the years, members of the U.S. Congress, both Republican and Democratic, have visited Taiwan. As described earlier, there has always been a strong positive sentiment in Congress to offer aid and comfort to the Taiwanese. While China has not been happy, it has pretty much sat back and done nothing. That changed when then–Speaker of the House Nancy Pelosi visited Taiwan in August 2022. When it was rumored that Pelosi intended to visit Taiwan's capital city of Taipei, China publicly reacted in the strongest diplomatic terms. Chinese leaders warned Pelosi to avoid visiting Taiwan on her scheduled trip to a number of Asian countries including Japan, one of America's key allies. Pelosi ignored the threats and visited with Taiwan's President Tsai Ing-wen, although shortly afterward the Biden Administration reaffirmed its decades-long One China policy. The Chinese were furious and showed it by carrying out several days of military maneuvers in the Taiwan Strait. China's response was greater in scale than any previous intimidation activities and served as proof of how much China's military capabilities had advanced since the 1996 Taiwan Strait Crisis. In April 2023, then–Speaker of the House Kevin McCarthy held a meeting with President Tsai Ing-wen in Southern California, where McCarthy promised his unwavering support for Taiwan. Support for Taiwan appears solid in the U.S. Congress at least for now, regardless of which political party has control.

ESCALATING FRUSTRATION

While China continues to ramp up its military capabilities and carry out incursions into Taiwanese territories, China is sophisticated enough to know that if it decided to invade Taiwan or seize the islands and atolls claimed by Taiwan, there would be an immediate worldwide reaction that could permanently damage China's political, military, and economic relationships with the United States and many other countries. All of this "Will-they-or-won't-they" has further served to bind together the United States and Japan as well as other countries in Southeast Asia. To the extent that China nevertheless decides to use its military power over a democratic Taiwan, what does this portend for other countries throughout the region?

Eventually we will learn how Russia's unprovoked and brutal invasion of Ukraine ultimately plays out. One result so far is that China and Russia have agreed to conduct joint military exercises over the next few years. What surprised Putin and his generals is that the Ukrainians were much more fierce and organized in responding to Russia's attack than expected, but even more importantly, Putin's war on the Ukraine led to a deeper unification of the countries comprising NATO and encouraged non-NATO countries to seek membership. This is clearly not the reaction Putin expected his invasion would trigger in the West. Xi Jinping will surely continue to carefully monitor events in Russia and Ukraine as they unfold in order to assess what could happen if China unilaterally decided to go beyond its Grey Zone strategies and accelerate its efforts to reunify Taiwan. This MaxTrend® will continue to frustrate Xi Jinping and Chinese leaders until China decides what it really wants.

CHAPTER SIX

DIGGING RARE EARTH ELEMENTS
(More than Just Microchips)

The global oil rush began quietly on August 27, 1859, when "Colonel" Edwin L. Drake from Titusville, Pennsylvania, struck oil at sixty-nine feet underground. One hundred sixty-five years later, as we evolve away from fossil fuels, rare earth elements are critical to the future of the world economy.

Chip technology is irreplaceable for advanced quantum computing, artificial intelligence, and other critical technologies. While chips themselves drive these technologies, there is something that is equally, if not more, fundamental than the chips themselves. At the heart of these technologies are rare earth elements. Consider basic cell phone technology. While the features and capabilities of smart phones continue to advance at lightning speed, these phones could not function at all without REEs. In short, REEs are irreplaceable for the proper operation of countless technologies we use in our everyday lives.

What are REEs? REEs are mineral materials that are extracted from refined ores.[1] There are infinite applications for even the most minute amounts of these minerals. For example, REEs are necessary for the proper functioning of aircraft engines, cell phones, hybrid car batteries, portable X-ray machines, lasers, MRI contrast agents—the list goes on. While some products and devices operate more efficiently with REEs as components, others simply will not operate at all without them. For example, lanthanum is a crucial component needed for manufacturing camera lenses, developing longer-running hybrid car batteries, and refining oil. Dysprosium is necessary for manufacturing nuclear reactor control rods and many types of lasers. Combining the REE neodymium with boron and iron results in producing powerful magnets that make cell phones, electric motors, and headphones operational.

It cannot be overemphasized that REEs are critical to the smooth operation of many industries and thus overall economies. This is why the ability to access REEs efficiently and reliably has become a matter of national security for many countries. The challenge is that the United States must import nearly all of its needed REEs because they are sourced outside the U.S.

Does the fact that the United States is importing most of its REEs mean that REEs are rare or not? The answer is confusing. In theory, REEs are not "rare" as far as the definition goes, because REEs can be found in ores located throughout Earth's crust, including some locations in the United States. The problem arises because REEs by their nature are mixed among other minerals in varying and imprecise concentrations. This means most REEs must be processed through multiple stages of treatment in order to achieve the desired concentration. Once a usable concentration is produced, another refiner extracts the high-purity elements that are then isolated from the contaminated materials. In the end, phosphors, alloys, oxides, and metals are extracted. Unfortunately, refining REEs is a highly toxic process requiring the application of powerful chemical solvents that are very damaging to the environment and will result in significant pollution.

CHINA AND RARE EARTH ELEMENTS

In the world of REEs, China finds itself in an enviable position for two reasons. First, while in theory REEs can be found all around the world, China can rightfully claim more than half of the world's known reserves.[2] Second, Chinese leaders more than twenty years ago implemented a national policy that targeted making China the global source of rare minerals. This was incredible foresight on China's part because, in recent years, the demand for REEs has rapidly expanded into new areas far beyond cell phone production.

China is the world's center for refining the REE extraction process: between 80 and 90 percent of the world's REEs are sourced there. But like everything in life, it comes at a cost. Refining has caused some areas of China to become highly toxic. One prime area is China's Jiangxi Province. Located about three hundred miles north of Hong Kong, the Jiangxi Province discovered high concentrations of certain REE ores over two decades ago. REE extraction quickly became a booming and highly profitable industry that, while economically beneficial, unfortunately resulted in harmful air, soil, and water pollution due to the refining processes.

It should come as no surprise that politics eventually entered the picture in regard to who controls these processes, to whom REEs are sold in the world marketplace, and where there is significant demand. It is more than just a matter of what buyer will pay the highest price. REEs have the potential to be used as a powerful political wedge by the Chinese. Confrontations have already occurred. On September 7, 2010, a Chinese trawler was near the Senkaku Islands south of Japan.[3] A Japanese ship and the Chinese trawler collided—apparently by accident—but China used this as an excuse to halt some shipments of REEs and specifically imposed export restrictions on REEs that had already been purchased by Japanese companies. With these sales blocked, the production capacities of several Japanese companies were severely curtailed. Another example is the Manganese Innovation Alliance. It is composed of most Chinese manganese producers, which reportedly control 90 percent of the world's manganese originating in China. The Alliance's ability to limit or control the sale of manganese poses a potential ongoing threat to Western buyers.

With the constantly looming specter of escalating political confrontations between the United States and China, the potential threat exists for China to cut off sales of REEs, and this has not been lost on the U.S. Department of Defense or U.S. intelligence agencies. Without question, America is vulnerable if China decides to refuse to export refined REEs to America or the West. In the short run, a cutoff of REEs would not immediately cripple the United States because the national defense stockpile located in Fort Belvoir, Virginia, maintains certain quantities of REEs. The idea of a government-maintained stockpile of metals dates back to World War I, when the U.S. became disadvantaged as critical commodities such as zinc, cobalt, and chromium became unavailable. However, those national stockpiles are not unlimited and would first be accessed for U.S. military purposes. If the stockpile were depleted, the impact on U.S. commercial markets would be extreme, and China would be in a strong position to use the threat of withholding REEs to counteract U.S. actions. This is similar to when the Biden Administration restricted the sale of certain microprocessors and microprocessor equipment to the Chinese in 2023.

The United States has begun responding to China's threats by encouraging the sourcing and extraction of REEs located domestically. While there are known reserves in California, Wyoming, Texas, and North Carolina, the problem remains that the ores containing REEs require a sophisticated and environmentally damaging refining process before the REEs are salable. While most Americans would agree with the importance of domestically sourcing its REEs, will elected government representatives be willing to stand behind and defend highly toxic refining taking place in their districts?

Admittedly, this MaxTrend® is an anomaly in that it seemingly favors China. In the REEs sector, China finds itself in a strong strategic position. However, the more China considers the withholding of REEs as a strategic threat, the more the United States and other countries are finding ways to lessen their dependence on Chinese sources. The

U.S. and other Western countries are capable of accessing REEs from sources other than China and developing their own processing facilities. While this will take time and money, REEs are no longer a card that China can play to its advantage.

CHAPTER SEVEN

THE ONE-TWO PUNCH OF BAD REAL ESTATE AND MANIPULATED CURRENCY

> Maxim 847: *Everything is worth what its purchaser will pay for it.*
> —Publilius Syrus, 42 BCE

Chances are you have never heard the name Publilius Syrus, but I will bet you have heard some of his sayings, among them "A rolling stone gathers no moss" (Maxim 524). Born in Antioch, Turkey, in 85 BCE, Syrus was transported to Rome as a slave where he eventually escaped his bonds and became a free man. Along the way, Syrus served as an improvisational actor for Julius Caesar, but he ultimately became famous for his many maxims (at the time known as sententiae). Syrus's maxim at the beginning of this chapter is one of the best and simplest summations of commerce. Today when describing what something is worth, we most often express it in terms of a specific currency (dollars, yen, euros, francs, pounds, renminbi, etc.). But in the end, the question is really more what the purchaser is willing to pay.

Xi Jinping is facing two MaxTrends® that represent serious road-blocks to China's struggling economy, which is no longer expanding at its astounding and historic 8 to 12 percent annual levels.[1] Both MaxTrends® (which are so closely intertwined that I'm covering them in the same chapter) could potentially derail Xi's ambitious goals for the year 2049—the one hundredth anniversary of the Chinese Communist Party.

The first MaxTrend® is China's dysfunctional real estate sector and how it is a very serious threat to China's economy. If China's residential and commercial real estate markets continue to fail, China's economy faces a rocky path. The second MaxTrend® is the fact that China's currency, the renminbi, is an outlier among the world's currencies. What I mean by that is the renminbi is a "nonhard" currency that is far different from the dollar, euro, pound, or yen, which are fully convertible and floating. Global trade depends on the ability to buy and sell goods and services freely. That is why offering to pay for something with a dollar, euro, yen, or pound is simple—banks around the world are familiar with those currencies and will easily complete the transaction. The renminbi is different in that its value is carefully monitored (controlled) by the Chinese central banking system. Payment in renminbi can be extremely difficult to convert into other currencies, and if you are paid in China, you may have to get permission from the Chinese government in order to move the funds out of China to convert. This makes dealing in renminbi complicated and inefficient. While at one point the Chinese could internally justify having a nonconvertible currency, that rationale no longer applies. Nevertheless, China refuses to cut the strings because it fears it would be unable to shield itself from external events in an open global economy.

A PRECURSOR: AMERICA'S REAL ESTATE BUBBLE

Unless you are younger than twenty-five, you personally experienced, or at least heard about, the 2007–2009 global financial crisis. It was the worst crash since the Great Depression hit in 1929, collapsing the world economy. The financial crisis of 2007–2009 was triggered by the subprime mortgage fiasco, which had its roots in the United States after 2002. Everyone back then could borrow money at fantastically low rates and then invest in real estate properties—what could go wrong? America's headlong rush into cheap interest rates led to a collapse in the U.S. that resulted in a severe liquidity crisis for the international financial system. Under severe strain, the market fell apart. At the heart of America's subprime mortgage crisis was greed. And, as the nursery rhyme goes, "All the king's horses and all the king's men couldn't put Humpty together again."

CHINA'S DYSFUNCTIONAL REAL ESTATE SECTOR

People everywhere have one thing in common—they can't resist a deal. This brings us to the People's Republic of China. Like America in the early 2000s, real estate offered an opportunity for China's rapidly burgeoning middle class to "get rich quick." Prior to the 1990s, private individuals could not own real estate in China because all real estate was owned by the state. That changed in the mid-1990s when it became possible for the average Chinese individual to "buy" real estate for the first time. What this really meant was that the Chinese (and some outsiders) were permitted to lease property from the Chinese government. Leases normally ran for 70 years with the expectation that those leases could be rolled over in the future. When this occurred, the prospect of buying an apartment or home was highly attractive to a rapidly growing and affluent Chinese middle class. Suddenly there was an incentive for Chinese individuals, couples, and families to invest their savings in real estate as they had probably already purchased all of the appliances and cars they needed or wanted. Real estate ownership in China took off like a rocket. Greed in China was not far behind—just like America.

Now, more than twenty-five years later, China is saddled with a dysfunctional real estate market. Three key elements can put this into perspective. First, between 25 and 33 percent of China's economy is tied up in the real estate sector. This represents a disproportionate amount of the Chinese economy in real estate that is owned by individuals. For a comparison, real estate in the United States makes up roughly 18 percent of the economy. Following the disastrous 2007–2009 subprime mortgage crash and bipartisan congressional action, the U.S. real estate market became much more tightly controlled than China's is today.

A second problem facing China is that about 70 percent of the assets owned by Chinese people as of 2023 were tied up in real estate. That is a very high percentage—and dangerous, because real estate assets by their nature are not liquid. Obviously, when real estate prices in China were booming, this was not a concern because an individual could simply collateralize loans against those real estate assets. China's problem today is that those real estate assets are underperforming and have been dropping in value over the last several years.

The third issue for Chinese regulators is that real estate development in China has been driven by private developers. This problem first received widespread public attention in 2021 when the China Evergrande Group, one of China's major private developers, became illiquid. This kicked off a panic in China as buyers who had put down large deposits for apartments not yet built found them not being delivered at all as Evergrande fell short of funds. Then, after losing $82 billion in 2021–22, Evergrande announced its inability to make payments to its creditors who were owed over $360 billion. In August 2023, Evergrande, after having seen its value plummet over the preceding two years, filed for bankruptcy in the United States, the Cayman Islands, and Hong Kong SAR to protect its few remaining assets and attempt to restructure.

Evergrande is not an isolated example. Another giant private Chinese real estate company, Country Garden, experienced similar problems throughout 2023. While Evergrande kicked off the real estate panic, Country Garden became a potentially even more serious threat to China's economy. In 2022, Country Garden was reportedly the largest private real estate developer in China—four times the size of Evergrande—handling more than one thousand projects throughout the country.

As early as 2020, Chinese regulators did try to get a handle on the emerging real estate problem, but they faced obstacles. One problem was that while Chinese officials can set rates and regulate certain parts of the officially sanctioned banking system, much of the money that went into financing the private real estate companies came from what are known as "shadow banks." Sometimes referred to as "trust companies," shadow banks are quasi-financial institutions only loosely regulated by Chinese officials. Shadow banks are where Chinese customers can deposit their savings in hopes of receiving much higher returns. For example, if a Chinese bank was paying 1 to 1.5 percent interest on customer deposits, the shadow banks might promise 6 percent, 7 percent, or more. Of course, investments by private individuals in those shadow banks are not guaranteed by the Chinese government. In 2023, Chinese shadow banks, including Zhongrong International Trust Co., Ltd., began experiencing equity problems. Potential failure of the shadow banks combined with too much money invested in real estate has truly shaken China's entire economy to the core. As of the time this chapter is being written, Xi Jinping has not elected to underwrite a bailout of China's private real estate sector. The cost of doing so would be tremendous (perhaps trillions of dollars) and would obligate the Chinese government to bail out private real estate developers whenever they got into trouble. It appears Chinese leaders are hoping that this mess will straighten itself out.

One thing to mention is that the Chinese government, even if it wanted to bail out the private real estate sector, faces a hard reality. While I am not an economist, there is a statistic of great importance called the "debt-to-GDP ratio." This ratio highlights a country's gross domestic product (GDP) in relation to exactly how much debt offsets it. America's debt-to-GDP ratio in 2023 was about 129 percent. Not a good sign for the U.S. economy when its debt exceeds its GDP, and this is one of the reasons some members of the U.S. Congress are vocal about America's high debt level. However, comparing the U.S.'s to China's debt-to-GDP ratio is eye-opening. In 2012, China's debt-to-GDP ratio was about 220 percent. Now, ten years later, during the period Xi Jinping has been managing China's economy, the ratio has risen to

297 percent. Any country, even one as large and centrally controlled as China, can juggle its debt structure for only so long without serious damage to the country's financial standing. All of this means that China faces ongoing and possibly insurmountable challenges because of its real estate mess.

THE RENMINBI: CHINA'S OUTLIER CURRENCY

China's main currency, the renminbi, presents a dilemma for Xi Jinping. On one hand, Xi's goal of transforming China into the world's dominant economic power is not truly achievable because China insists on maintaining a nonconvertible currency that remains an outlier among other global currencies such as the yen, dollar, euro, and pound. On the other hand, by strictly controlling the convertibility of the renminbi, China for decades has been able to give a significant competitive advantage to the hundreds of thousands of Chinese companies manufacturing products for the export markets. This balancing act continues, but it is turning less favorable for China.

It helps to briefly describe how China's monetary system is structured. China's currency is denoted as either the renminbi (RMB) or the yuan (CNY). Technically, the renminbi is the official currency of China and acts as the actual medium of exchange (in the same way the dollar serves as America's medium of exchange). The yuan is the unit of account used by China's government within the Chinese financial system. For our purposes, though, think of the yuan and the renminbi as interchangeable. Only true economists really care to differentiate between the two.

The world's current financial structure had its roots in the 1930s during the Great Depression, when global trade and commerce ground to a halt. The nearly total devastation wrought by World War II then drove the world economy to its knees. When it became clear in 1944 that the Western Allies would eventually defeat both Germany and Japan, political and economic representatives from forty-four countries—in a truly rare example of international cooperation—gathered together in

Bretton Woods, New Hampshire. There, at the height of World War II, world leaders and financial experts worked together to hammer out a new global financial and trade system intended to jumpstart the world economy postwar. The resulting Bretton Woods Agreement was a landmark accomplishment because it created a revolutionary system designed to foster monetary and global exchange. Bretton Woods established the International Monetary Fund (IMF), which eventually became the World Bank Group. Its goal was simple—rescue troubled world economies and make all global currencies fully convertible to make international trade possible.

The big winner in the currency race over the last seventy-five years has been the United States. Since the 1940s, the U.S. dollar has been designated as the primary reserve currency for the rest of the world. Initially this was possible because the value of the U.S. dollar was directly tied to the price of gold. The "gold standard" worked on and off until 1971 when, to the surprise of economists, President Nixon abruptly decoupled the U.S. dollar from the price of gold. Nixon acted because he was worried that more dollars were being held outside the United States by non-U.S. entities, and those dollars exceeded the total gold reserves held in the U.S. (in locations such as Fort Knox). Nevertheless, even after the delinking of the U.S. dollar and gold, the global trading system has continued to use the dollar as the primary global reserve currency. This was possible as the world's currencies (such as the dollar, the pound, the franc, and others) were allowed to "float"; that is, periodically adjust to each other, creating a more stable global economy.

China was an outlier in that it instead strictly pegged the value of its renminbi to the U.S. dollar and refused to permit the renminbi to float regardless of China's financial circumstances (which were depressed for decades). After the CCP gained control of China in 1949, leader Mao Zedong for the next quarter century imposed a policy in which totally centralized government decision-making ruled China. This policy created severe repercussions in that the Chinese economy remained severely depressed for decades. At the time it was not viewed as important because China's interaction with the rest of the world was insignificant in terms of trade. But as China's economy expanded explosively during the late 1980s, 1990s, and into the 2000s, China's customers and competitors around the world became concerned and then upset that Chinese officials were managing (or, in harsher terms, manipulating) China's currency to their own benefit. Under tremendous international political pressure, China in July 2015 switched from its strictly fixed exchange rates to a more hybrid floating exchange rate for the renminbi. That concession, however, is misleading, because the actual range and time periods in which the Chinese permit the renminbi to fluctuate are extremely small.

CURRENCY MANIPULATION

Why does the rest of the world care that China's renminbi is so closely tied to the U.S. dollar? The reason is simple. Until the last ten years, China was primarily an export-driven economy, manufacturing components and products for nearly every country in the world. This enabled China to vault over its competitors until today, when it boasts the second largest economy next to the United States. By self-adjusting the rate of the renminbi, Chinese officials were able to suppress the prices at which it sold exported goods. Basically, lowering the value of the renminbi depressed export prices, which made Chinese goods far more competitive than might otherwise have been the case. For nearly four decades, this practice enabled China to amass trillions of dollars in foreign currency reserves in dollars, euros, francs, pounds, and yen, which China has used to rapidly upgrade its economy. Even when in 2015 the International Monetary Fund declared the yuan an official "reserve currency," the Chinese nevertheless retained control of its overall value. China's Central Bank still carefully monitors the peg at which the U.S. dollar is set to the yuan. If the dollar value versus the renminbi goes above the peg, China's Central Bank has the option to sell U.S. treasuries it holds in the secondary market, which in effect lowers the value of the yuan.

Currency manipulation has been a charge leveled against the Chinese for years. In 2019, former president Trump actually designated China as a "currency manipulator." It is important to recognize though, that U.S. consumers do benefit directly from a lower-valued yuan because much of what China exports to the United States—cell phones, computers, toys, sporting goods, apparel—is valued in the billions. The other side of the coin is that while the American consumer may benefit, the trade deficit between China and the United States has exploded exponentially over the last twenty to thirty years. This is one reason why China remains one of the largest holders of U.S. treasury bonds.

A CURRENCY CONUNDRUM

For years, China has been able to manage the value of its renminbi as a way to promote its export-driven economy. But in recent years, as China has begun to move away from its reputation for exports and wants to be recognized as more of a global leader, it faces increasing international pressures to allow the renminbi to become a more desirable (convertible) currency for other countries to accept. In order to do this, the value of the renminbi should be permitted to float freely and join a flexible exchange system like most other leading global currencies. However, Xi Jinping nevertheless insists on maintaining a top-down management of China's economy; thus, his challenge will be to decide whether the economy would benefit from a market-determined flexible exchange rate or if China should retain an artificially manipulated outlier currency. In the long run, a flexible renminbi might benefit China, but the short run is not so clear, partially because of Xi's efforts to carefully manipulate all aspects of China's economy.

Why is China so afraid of floating its currency? In terms of the average Chinese investor, while most have overinvested in real estate in China, many would prefer to purchase foreign assets (including real estate) and currencies to spread their investment risks. The reality facing Chinese government officials is that if the renminbi becomes a truly convertible currency, China will experience a large outflow of its capital from its borders that would be difficult for Chinese regulators to stem. Wealthy Chinese will seek attractive and profitable places outside of China to invest their money. Exporters too would find themselves encouraged to hold less funds in renminbi and to convert the rest into other international currencies. And to the extent the money goes overseas, China's banks and government officials will have far less control over where those funds are invested. In short, the Chinese government would no longer be able to exercise such strictly controlled top-down management of China's economy.

If Chinese private investors were able to move their money abroad, then Chinese banks would find themselves at risk. During the Asian economic crash of 2008 to 2010, China was relatively protected from the financial downslide because most of the holdings of Chinese companies and investors were in renminbi and essentially locked up in China. If during the crisis China had been able to easily convert renminbi into foreign currencies, the Chinese government would have had far greater problems. On the other hand, foreign exchange is important for Chinese companies as they desire to become global players with business activities not just within China but around the world. Having an inconvertible currency makes this much more difficult.

Even though China's exchange regime over the years has slowly transformed from a fully fixed to a semifixed to a more flexible rate, the permissible range for adjustment between the U.S. dollar and the renminbi remains very narrow. In the end, the only way China can fix this is to have transparency in its policies that is communicated to the global market. I have little doubt that this and China's overreliance on real estate investments presents a serious challenge that keeps Xi Jinping and his financial advisors awake at night.

CHAPTER EIGHT

A FRACTURED GLOBAL SUPPLY CHAIN THREATENS CHINA

If there is one single factor most responsible for China's meteoric rise from a backwater economy to the second most powerful nation in the world, it is China's massive manufacturing base and nationwide infrastructure of ports, railroads, highways, airports, and industrial parks. China as a premier manufacturing center exports countless parts, components, supplies, and finished products to customers around the globe. Being at the center of the global supply chain for nearly three decades has brought trillions of dollars, yen, euros, and other foreign currencies into China and financed impressive growth and new infrastructure. Now, the permanent fracturing of the global supply chain threatens China's economic future. Though COVID-19 contributed somewhat, the real causes are many—rising labor costs, decreasing foreign investment, cyber warfare, politics, and increased competition from other countries.

Let me begin this chapter with a true story about the supply chain. By the fall of 2020, COVID-19 had overtaken the United States after having ravaged China, parts of Europe, and much of Asia. At that time, I was asked to help a company located in northern New Jersey that sells a type of "black box" comprised of numerous components. Each unit sells for about US$1,400 to customers that incorporate it into a larger electronic device. The problem was that the New Jersey company had one thousand of these units gathering dust in a warehouse because they were waiting on a single key component. This necessary component was sole-sourced out of China and had a per unit value of about US$32. While the Chinese supplier continuously promised delivery, it was late by 30, 60, 90+ days, all while sending emails demanding the U.S. company pay "in advance" for the parts. Feeling something was off, I asked a contact in China to investigate by visiting this Chinese supplier—and that is how I learned that the factory had long been shut down and abandoned. This particular case was resolved by purchasing a 3D printer and producing the missing part in New Jersey, but similar situations have arisen thousands of times since the pandemic broke out.

The global supply chain as we know it is irretrievably broken. Nothing will ever again be "normal." This MaxTrend® has far-reaching implications for nations, government leaders, businesses, investors, and individual consumers everywhere, but particularly for China.

Those who believe that COVID-19 was solely responsible for the fracturing of the global supply chain are mistaken. The truth is that COVID-19 merely accelerated a transformation that was already underway well before 2020. There are a number of diverse factors responsible for the radical transformations of the supply chain. This chapter explains how the global supply chain collapsed and then examines those underlying factors that led to where we are today. All will directly influence the success or failure of China and Xi Jinping's goals.

WHERE WE WERE

The global supply chain was already visibly cracking under external pressures prior to January 2020. In a sense, the coronavirus striking China simply acted as an accelerant. The outbreak in Wuhan (regardless of why and how the virus mutated) was a perfect storm of timing and location.

The most widely celebrated holiday in China is the Chinese New Year, which takes place in late January and early February. Basically, during the nearly two-week-long celebration, all of China's industry literally shuts down. Roughly 500+ million Chinese citizens travel throughout the country, most returning to their home provinces to celebrate with family.[1] This means that while the coronavirus was quietly beginning to spread in early 2020, a half billion people were traveling across China by trains, planes, and automobiles for the New Year festivities. It was during these two weeks that the coronavirus outbreak exploded. Any other time of year it might have been isolated in just one or two regions, but because of the heavy holiday travel, the virus quickly spread throughout all of China. As a result, when Chinese factories were scheduled to restart production in early February 2020, they didn't. Millions of workers were either sick or stranded in distant locations, and so tens of thousands of factories shut down because at least half of their workforce wasn't available. This created an unantici-pated and serious dislocation for China's entire economy during the first and second quarters of 2020.

The *South China Morning Post*, one of Hong Kong's premier news outlets, published an explosive article in April 2020 stating that during the first quarter of 2020, 460,000 Chinese companies had closed as a result of the coronavirus. The Chinese government was furious with the reporting but could do little once the story was out. A high percentage of those Chinese companies were engaged in contract manufacturing for products destined for export to customers located around the world. Thus, during the first two quarters of 2020, the Chinese economy severely contracted. To put that into perspective, the Chinese government had not reported a contraction in China's economy since 1976 (the year Mao Zedong died after ruling China for decades). Forty-four years of unabated economic growth came to a dramatic halt between January and June 2020. The sudden closure and slow reopening of Chinese factories in 2020 disrupted the production of consumer goods, components, assemblies for manufacturers, and unique items produced for companies around the world and Chinese industries themselves.

Then, during the summer of 2020, as China slowly began to reopen, the economies of first Europe and then North America shut down as the COVID-19 virus spread. The ripple effect continued and the global economy was depressed during 2020 and into 2021. Ports, particularly on America's West Coast such as Long Beach, Los Angeles, San Francisco, and Seattle, ground to a halt, and hundreds of ships waiting to unload their cargo from China were backed up for weeks and sometimes months. Some trans-Pacific container ships that tried to avoid the West Coast congestion by rerouting through the Panama Canal to the East Coast of the United States ended up experiencing the same problems and delays. If you looked at only these factors, you could understandably conclude that the global supply chain breakdown was caused by the pandemic. However, more fundamental factors were at play in the background.

THE FALLACY OF "JUST-IN-TIME" MANUFACTURING

Around 1985, Japanese companies became extremely aggressive in pursuing international opportunities. This was Japan experiencing its "bubble period." As the Japanese economy grew explosively between 1985 and 1992, some self-styled experts believed Japan was poised to take over the world. That, of course, didn't happen, but Japanese companies at the time believed it and began acquiring properties and setting up manufacturing outlets across the globe. Particularly prevalent were Japanese automobile manufacturers such as Toyota, which began establishing integrated manufacturing facilities throughout the United States. A corporate philosophy often attributed to Toyota was operating by a system whereby manufacturers would order parts and components "just in time" to be put into their assembly lines. The appeal was that significant cost savings could be realized by not tying up capital in inventory. For a while, the just-in-time philosophy worked well for Japanese companies and their key suppliers. Seeing this success led some leading consulting firms in the U.S. to recommend the concept to their American clients. Just-in-time sounded simple and foolproof—manufacturers simply needed to sign contracts with suppliers so that when parts or components were needed, they were immediately delivered. What could go wrong? Soon, just-in-time manufacturing became the mantra for many American and European companies. This coincided with the time when labor in China was extremely inexpensive. Thus, the same consultants advised American and European companies to seek out the lowest labor cost manufacturing locations, which at the time meant China. Because top-level executives are always looking to save money, this led to a boom period for China as its government-funded special economic zones spread throughout the country and attracted manufacturing outsourced from the United States and Europe.

For nearly three decades, it looked like everything was going according to plan. Just-in-time manufacturing was working like a dream. Companies from the United States and Europe outsourced more and more of their manufacturing needs to factories in China and later to Thailand, the Philippines, Malaysia, and elsewhere throughout Southeast Asia. The unrecognized reality during those three decades, as China greatly benefited from a supply chain based on just-in-time manufacturing, was that Chinese labor was becoming much more expensive and thus less competitive. Since the rationale behind just-in-time sourcing depended on cheap labor, that started the ground shaking. Even as some companies moved out of China to other locations beginning as early as 2012, labor rates continued to rise throughout all of Asia.

SEEING THROUGH THE MANUFACTURED REASONS

While not outwardly obvious prior to 2020, China for years had faced serious challenges impacting its economy. This did not come to a head until COVID-19 arrived and it became clear how these challenges created a drag on China's manufacturing industries, ultimately affecting the global supply chain. Nine major issues contributed to this.

- The first was the widespread and rapidly growing environmental crisis in China. One direct result of China's extensive development of special economic zones (SEZs) to house manufacturing companies was that China had been (and still is) suffering from widespread air pollution and a lack of potable water throughout the country. This greatly affected how Chinese companies were able to operate in an increasingly competitive environment. The human and health costs for China have been severe.

- Beginning in 1985 and for the next twenty-five years, China had very little serious competition as it aggressively exported products globally through manufacturers in its SEZs. However, other countries in Southeast Asia have over the last ten years emerged as more aggressive and effective regional competitors. Those potential competitors pointed to problems in China as a good reason why foreign companies needing inexpensive and reliable suppliers should look to other options throughout Southeast Asia. While India has been slow to the party, it is quickly starting to catch up as an alternative to China.

- In the past, Chinese workers were efficient while being very low paid. That has changed significantly. While Chinese workers are still not paid at the level of most American or European laborers, promoting China as a "cheap" place to manufacture is no longer true. This encourages multinationals to consider other less expensive countries in which to do business.

- For years China has been concerned about a debt crisis experienced by Chinese banks and financial institutions.

Many of these problems took place at the provincial levels where local financial institutions lent funds to less than top-quality borrowers. This debt crisis continues to impact China's economy at both the provincial and national levels.

- As part of the Chinese private lending boom, thousands of residential housing projects and planned communities were approved and funded throughout China's provinces. Much of this construction was completed with financing without the oversight (or in some cases, approval) of the Chinese government. Because too many projects were speculatively funded, there are now numerous unoccupied housing and commercial projects creating a drag on China's economy.

- A demographic challenge facing China is its aging workforce. Many might be surprised to learn that the average retirement age in China is fifty-four. For women working in blue-collar jobs, the retirement age is often even younger. Because of the dwindling population due to decades of the government-enforced one-child policy, industries throughout China are experiencing serious labor shortages. This is exacerbated by the fact that people are living longer, thus creating long-term social support obligations.

- China still faces the threat of political unrest in Tibet, Western China, and Hong Kong SAR. This makes it more challenging for foreign companies to conduct business in and with China. As explained elsewhere in this book, foreign governments are imposing restrictions on what products can be sourced from Chinese companies in certain regions.

- Under the Trump Administration, tariff and trade wars involving the United States and Europe became a much higher priority. The same policy has continued under the Biden Administration. China, which for decades had run very high trade deficits with the U.S. and other countries, is being targeted by those governments seeking a better balance.

SOURCES OF THE GLOBAL SUPPLY CHAIN CRISIS

As described throughout this book, MaxTrends® is the word I use to identify developments and events that of themselves impact nations and in some cases the entire global economy. There are at least six MaxTrends® that are accelerating the fracturing of the global supply chain.

RISING GLOBAL LABOR COSTS. During the 1970s, the U.S. economy was booming and labor rates increased across the board. There was a point in the 1970s when skilled manufacturing costs in the United States were twenty to twenty-five times higher than they were in China. Of course, that was a time when China was not engaged in manufacturing for the export sector and had a backward agrarian economy. China began to build up its manufacturing capacity in the 1980s by establishing SEZs, first in Southern China and then moving up the coast. China invested massive amounts of capital to construct infrastructure in the form of railroads, ports, and highways that would be vital to Chinese companies seeking global markets. Then in the 1980s, Japanese companies (as most clearly espoused by Toyota) began to talk up the concept of "just-in-time" manufacturing, which caught the attention of major consulting organizations such as Boston Consulting Group, McKinsey & Company, and others. The race was then on for U.S. companies that saw the financial advantages of no longer carrying large inventories of parts and components but instead using just-in-time as a justification for offshoring their manufacturing needs. This led to an avalanche of U.S. companies rushing to offshore production to China, particularly because China had constructed the infrastructure to support it. This continued for decades until the trade deficit between China and the United States grew so large (over $300 billion a year) that it captured the attention of politicians in America as well as in Europe. As the relationship between China and the United States became more strained, economists and politicians began to realize that Chinese labor was no longer cheap. This drove some foreign companies to move out of China or at least second-source elsewhere in Southeast Asia. This MaxTrend® continues today as labor costs around the world continue to rise and the original rationale of "It's cheaper to make it overseas" is no longer as true as it once was.

CYBER WARFARE. Cyber warfare is being utilized by many governments around the world, including China and the United States. It is no longer a matter of a government entity looking to surreptitiously obtain information. The global supply chain is particularly vulnerable to cyberattacks. While the cyber activities of Russia, North Korea, and Iran are well known, those of China have been less publicized. But make no mistake—China is deliberately using cyber techniques to obtain key technologies from non-Chinese companies. There have already been a number of publicized cases in which the U.S. government has indicted Chinese actors for illegal cyber activities. China as the second largest economy in the world and a highly sophisticated cyber player will largely determine how well or how poorly the global economy is affected by these activities in the coming years.

3D MANUFACTURING. Although not everyone realizes it, 3D manufacturing (also known as 3D printing or additive manufacturing) has already come of age. It is no longer a technology that is limited by its original use, which was producing prototypes. Beginning in the 1980s, creating prototypes for evaluation and suitability (which are always expensive to produce) was greatly enhanced by the use of primitive 3D printers that allowed companies to produce these prototypes inexpensively. 3D technology then expanded much more quickly than was originally predicted. Today, major global companies such as Boeing are investing enormous amounts to research how additive manufacturing can be used to create better sources for specialized aeronautics components. The extent that 3D plants with server farms permit larger-scale manufacturing output (as opposed to one-by-one production) has already affected the global economy and will have the greatest impact on China. Why? Because while 3D manufacturing and printing are still costly when large numbers of components are required, it is quickly becoming much less expensive. On top of that, the ability to eliminate transportation costs and shipping delays (which are built into the current supply chain structure) will become increasingly attractive to companies like Boeing. This will hurt China because its exports to the Americas or to Europe will become less cost competitive. 3D manufacturing will also encourage companies to reengineer their lines of existing products to contain fewer components and thus become less expensive and more efficient to produce.

ROBOTICS. The use of robots, and particularly robots combined with increasingly powerful artificial intelligence (AI), is a truly historic development that will change how the global supply chain functions. As mentioned throughout this book, China has benefited for decades from relying on its inexpensive labor force. Robotics is a game changer. As safety in the workplace becomes an increasing priority, robotics makes manufacturing not only more efficient but much safer overall. A good example is that of robot palletizers incorporating 360° AI vision systems that can produce both increased efficiencies and more predictable safety protocols. While robots and AI were very expensive during their inception, the costs of implementation are coming down rapidly. This has already had a direct impact on supply chain logistics. During the COVID-19 crisis, consumers worldwide became accustomed to ordering items and expecting quick or near-immediate delivery. The ability to meet these demands was accelerated by robotics. Robotics is a MaxTrend® that China will either have to embrace or risk falling behind.

FOREIGN DIRECT INVESTMENT. Beginning in the early 1980s, and particularly as China was opening up as a manufacturing center, the Chinese government was extremely liberal in encouraging inbound foreign investment. China was desperate for hard currencies (dollars, yen, euros, and francs) that Chinese leaders could recycle into funding infrastructure growth. China had to attract hard currencies because its national currency, the renminbi, was not fully convertible. While foreign direct investment (FDI) greatly spurred the growth of the Chinese economy, some breaks in the momentum occurred, such as during the Asian financial crisis (July 1997 to December 1998). Even throughout that crisis, though, China suffered less than other economies.

After the 1997 Asian financial crisis ended, China continued to seek out foreign investment until the next financial crisis hit between mid-2007 and early 2009. That particular meltdown led to serious harm not just in Asian countries but also the United States as America's housing bubble exploded. U.S. housing prices, which had been on an upward path, began to rapidly decline, and in 2007 U.S. home sales experienced their largest drop in more than twenty years. This was a result of the faulty subprime mortgage industry. First, the investment bank Bear Stearns collapsed and was quickly rescued by JPMorgan Chase in a transaction backed by the U.S. government. This was followed by the Lehman Brothers Holdings bankruptcy and the subsequent government-backed rescue of the American International Group (AIG), which was then the largest insurer in the United States and facing insolvency. Upon taking office, former president Barack Obama stopped the bleeding by signing a stimulus package into law. Yet again, during this trying period for the world economy, China suffered less than most other industrialized nations.

What went largely unnoticed then is that during this period the Chinese leadership became less interested in attracting inbound foreign direct investment and more focused on tightening its internal policies. This restriction on foreign investment in China emerged as a key policy promoted by Xi Jinping. Since 2013, the Chinese government has increasingly monitored the activities of foreign companies operating in China (as well as major Chinese companies), a policy that accelerated during the Trump Administration. Like China, other nations over the last several years, including the United States, Britain, France, Germany, and Japan, have initiated their own closer looks at foreign direct investment and what kinds of projects they will monitor and potentially block in terms of perceived national security risk. This MaxTrend® continues to accelerate.

POLITICS. Since the COVID-19 outbreak, governments around the world have been demanding more domestic sourcing, and there are a number of reasons for this. First, the concept of national security has become a much higher priority. The pandemic triggered a review of how governments sourced medical equipment and protective gear when hospitals were overrun with patients and dangerously low on supplies. Next, governments are aware of the need to combat high unemployment rates among younger workers, because failing to do so leads to political unrest and economic instability. Then, as the supply chain continues to fracture and basic consumer items become increasingly difficult to obtain, governments feel the pressure to fix the problems before they boil over. These political obstacles, be they in the United States, China, the European Union, or Africa, are universal. Governments are being pressured to make their economies, and thus their constituents, less subject to the whims of external events. The global supply chain, which is dependent on moving massive amounts of products around the world, will continue to be a primary concern of politicians everywhere.

RUSSIA INVADES UKRAINE

Aside from the MaxTrends® described above, random unexpected events can and will continue to significantly impact how the global supply chain operates. The best recent example of this is Russia's unprovoked attack on Ukraine in February 2022. When Russia invaded Ukraine, the global supply chain was immediately affected. Like COVID-19, Russia's invasion acted as another accelerant of the MaxTrends® that were already affecting global trade patterns. Eight direct impacts on the supply chain were felt in the months following Russia's attack on Ukraine.

IMPACT 1: A critical shortage of key metals quickly developed. Supplies of metals such as palladium, aluminum, titanium, nickel, and lithium were disrupted because those metals are sourced from the Ukraine regions invaded by Russia. One prime example is palladium. Palladium is an essential metal widely used in manufacturing catalytic converters for automobiles, and more than 50 percent of the world's palladium comes from Russia and Ukraine.

IMPACT 2: The basic idea behind China's Belt and Road Initiative was to construct a physical network to ship products overland between China and Europe, which would be much more efficient and profitable than transporting by container ships around Africa or through the Suez Canal. Some land-based trade routes have been built between China and Europe; however, Russia's invasion of Ukraine has disrupted the reliability of those routes.

IMPACT 3: The worldwide automobile industry was immediately impacted by the Ukraine invasion, particularly for those European manufacturers that had before the war assembled and sourced significant vehicle components from Ukraine. The collapse of the Ukrainian economy directly impacted their production capabilities.

IMPACT 4: Air transportation between Russia and Europe abruptly stopped, and this continues to disrupt portions of the supply chain.

IMPACT 5: After the initial attack on Ukraine, sea routes via the Black Sea were disrupted. Turkey's control of the Bosporus Strait became politicized, further complicating the situation.

IMPACT 6: Until the invasion, Ukraine was one of the world's agricultural powerhouses. Because significant amounts of wheat, corn, and sunflower crops were not planted due to the Russian invasion, shortages of key foodstuffs resulted and directly drove up prices. Africa was particularly affected.

IMPACT 7: Energy prices remain unpredictable.

IMPACT 8: Global financial transactions were disrupted as Russian banking and financial institutions were cut off. This has slowed payments and money transfers globally.

CHAIN REACTION

The collapse of the global supply chain continues to affect everyone everywhere, and one of the countries most susceptible is China. We need to keep our eye on China to see how it responds to these challenges. Watch for two particular developments. First, internal politics will increasingly dominate China's policy on external engagements. For example, if China decides to take aggressive action against Taiwan, this decision will massively damage the global supply chain. Second, it is clear that the just-in-time manufacturing theory is outdated, if for no other reason than labor, particularly Chinese labor, is no longer inexpensive. Thus, companies will be forced to decide whether it still makes sense to sole-source products from politically difficult areas such as China.

The bottom line is that the global supply chain will never return to business as usual. All eyes should remain on China. Without a strong export sector, China's overall economy will suffer. China's response to all of the factors affecting the global supply chain will have an outsized impact on the world and China itself.

CHAPTER NINE

WORSENING CLIMATE CHANGE AND POLLUTING POLICIES

On June 15, 2022, massive floods inundated much of Bangladesh, putting millions of homes underwater. These were reportedly the worst floods to strike the country in over one hundred years. Home to nearly 170 million people, Bangladesh is a low-lying country that is regularly plagued by cyclones, floods, and hurricanes. However, in recent years, things have gone from bad to worse. According to a division of the United Nations, over the next ten years, if global warming continues, 20 percent of the population of Bangladesh will need to be relocated, at enormous human and financial costs.

According to a division of the United Nations, climate change, along with its life-altering repercussions, is the defining issue of this generation. The harsh truth is that massive climactic changes are affecting every corner of our planet; Bangladesh is not an outlier. China is equally at risk. As weather patterns become increasingly erratic and severe, widespread physical damage, loss of life, and threats to worldwide food production are just some of the results we can expect. The consequences are inescapable.

While the extent of climate change is not yet uniformly spread around the world, every country is experiencing some measurable increase in its average temperatures. In short, our planet is getting noticeably and dangerously warmer. While weather patterns are by nature constantly evolving, rapid fluctuations have been recorded since the 1800s. Think about it. The human population has grown over the last two hundred years, while simultaneously the factories born of the

Industrial Revolution have been releasing greenhouse gases that, simply put, trap the sun's heat within the Earth's atmosphere.

Carbon dioxide and methane are the two most significant contributors to global warming. Since the 1880s, the average global temperature has risen by about 1.1 degrees centigrade. This may sound insignificant, but it is not. While we have seen some smaller variations between 2011 and 2021, the world today is experiencing its warmest temperatures in recorded history. The most visible manifestations of this are melting polar ice caps and glaciers, rising sea levels, an increase in wildfires due to intense droughts, shrinking rivers, and water scarcity. While every country is being affected to some degree by climate change, China is particularly vulnerable. In the next chapter, the harmful effects of air pollution in China, particularly on children, are discussed, along with the chronic shortage of water throughout China, most notably in the northern regions.

One of the less visible but equally concerning results of higher global temperatures is a shocking decline in biodiversity, as growing numbers of plant and animal species struggle to survive. Most experts concur that to avoid catastrophe, we must prevent the planet's average temperature from increasing more than 1.5 degrees centigrade through the end of this century. While a moderation in temperatures will not avoid climate impacts, it can at least serve to make the overall global temperatures more bearable.

It should come as no surprise that the ten most industrialized nations[1] are responsible for nearly 70 percent of the emissions leading to climate change. Again, not surprisingly, fossil fuels are one of the major causes of global warming. Under the leadership of the United Nations, the goal is to reach net zero emissions by the year 2050, with the hope that at least half of the world's current emissions will be reduced by 2030 in order to keep global warming below the 1.5 degrees centigrade mark. Is this realistically achievable? No one knows.

CHINA AND THE ENVIRONMENT

Global warming is a problem that China should have no choice but to address because of the massive emissions generated by China's industrial sector. If China fails to adopt wide-ranging and effective policies, the future of the world is bleak, regardless of what measures other nations take. This has not gone unnoticed by Xi Jinping and the current Chinese leadership, especially when on January 13, 2013, Beijing recorded the worst level of air pollution in its history. That pervasive and deadly smog directly affected more than 600 million Chinese citizens, many of whom experienced serious short- and long-term respiratory illnesses as a result. This occurred just two months after Xi Jinping was elected the general secretary of the Communist Party Central Committee at the 18th National Congress of the Chinese Communist Party, the moment when Xi officially entered the world stage for the first time as China's leader.

It is no secret that none of Xi Jinping's predecessors seriously addressed the topic of climate change. Xi, though, had no choice when, barely sixty days after taking office, he was confronted with the most daunting environmental crisis in China's history. To his credit, Xi correctly recognized that his failure to respond would result in significant long-term domestic implications. Xi's predecessors over the prior three decades had aggressively pursued policies aimed at catching China up with the world's more industrialized nations; they were not prioritizing (nor did they seem to care about) the environmental impact. Coal was their choice of energy source to drive China's industrial growth. However, the repercussions of their dependence on coal are still being felt today. To put this into perspective, in 2019 (according to the U.S. Environmental Protection Agency), the United States released about 6.6 billion tons of harmful carbon dioxide (CO_2) into the atmosphere. That in itself is a significant amount. But during that same year, China released over 13 billion tons of CO_2—almost twice as much. With coal still providing energy for nearly two-thirds of China's factories, 21 percent of CO2 levels come from China's massive steel industry, and 30 percent come from construction emissions.

THE PARIS ACCORD

Two years after the record-breaking Beijing smog event, Xi Jinping decided that China should become a signatory to the Paris Accord (also known as the Paris Agreement), which was drafted on December 12, 2015, to establish long-term goals for all nations of the world to counteract harmful climate change. A legally binding treaty, the Paris Accord came into effect on November 4, 2016, and as of today has been ratified by 195 countries. Each signatory to the Paris Accord is expected to set its own goals and is then given five years in which to achieve those goals. This will continue to be Xi Jinping's challenge. In international agreements, the Chinese often adopt the strategy of overpromising on their obligations. In the Paris Accord, China seems to follow this same pattern. China in 2016 promised that its national carbon dioxide emissions would peak before the year 2030, and that China would become carbon neutral by 2060. While it is a hopeful sign that China publicly acknowledged climate change as a serious problem, Xi Jinping is the sole individual with the power to ensure China keeps its promises.

Here is the problem. Again, China has been the world's largest emitter of CO2 gases since 2006. The reason is because coal makes up two-thirds of China's energy consumption. Coal burning in China through coal-fired power stations, coal mining, and blast furnaces producing iron and steel is responsible for 27 percent of the world's total carbon dioxide emissions. This means that if China falls short on its promises under the Paris Accord, there is no way the rest of the world can effectively reverse the rise of global carbon dioxide levels. China promised in 2016 to halt the construction of new coal-fired plants for two years, but when the ban expired in 2018, China began building new coal plants. China even today is building coal plants at a rate three times faster than the rest of the world.

China's high energy demands are really no mystery. Over the last half century China has radically transformed itself from a largely agricultural to a more industrialized and urban society. As more and more Chinese migrate each year from rural areas to cities, demands for new construction, housing, cement, rebar, steel, roads, cars, and electrical grids grow. Xi Jinping has publicly spoken about this at various international conferences while stressing that China is serious about reversing climate change. Aside from promises to achieve carbon neutrality by 2060, China has stated that it plans to convert to renewable energy sources so as to account for 25 percent of its consumption by 2030. To that end, Xi has encouraged the installation of solar and wind power generators throughout China with the goal of generating a combined capacity of over 1.2 billion kilowatts by 2030. Along with this, China is undertaking the reforestation of green areas that have been depleted in the past as a natural way of reducing carbon dioxide. The real concern is that even if China achieves its promised goals, it is not enough, because China will still remain the world's largest emitter of greenhouse gases.

CHINA'S GLOBAL REPUTATION

While climate change with its implications is a constant threat for countries around the world, it is a uniquely significant challenge for China and its reputation. Over the last ten years, China has sought to assume a global leadership role in a variety of areas. China's ambition is to become the global representative of all countries throughout the developing world. This places additional pressure on China to take stronger and more positive steps to limit its CO2 emissions, because other countries, like Vietnam, India, and

Indonesia, have made more significant commitments of their own under the Paris Accord.

Yet, China still consumes more coal than the entire rest of the world and continues to build coal-fired plants. While it is true that some of the new plants will replace older, more inefficient ones, the problem is that coal-fired plants have a life cycle of thirty to forty years. This timeframe has the potential to negate China's carbon-neutrality deadline. With coal providing over 55 percent of the energy used in China, China's massive overdependence on coal seriously brings into question whether China can in fact meet its obligations under the Paris Accord. Aside from coal, China still struggles with serious levels of air pollution. It is not forgotten by Chinese leadership that the widespread outrage over the 2013 Beijing air pollution reports forced the Chinese government to take more aggressive actions to combat the underlying causes.

There is some hope. China today is the largest consumer of electric vehicles (EVs). In 2022, about 26 percent of the vehicles sold in China were EVs. But while this is a positive trend, the total number of EVs still comprise only a small percentage of the more than 250 million vehicles on China's roads. Xi Jinping will face increased internal political pressure if the growing problems with China's air pollution continue to pose health risks.

China for years has been pushing its ambitious Belt and Road Initiative. One of the major bullet points of the Belt and Road Initiative was the promise China made to finance coal-fired plants in other countries. China's announcement that it will continue to build coal-fired plants in China but cease financing them around the world is a step in the right direction (though whether this actually comes about will be interesting to see). It is encouraging news that China is pushing hard for solar- and wind-powered generation. However, the truth is that for China to truly lessen its dependence on coal, solar and wind are not enough.

While a highly controversial global issue is the future of nuclear power, China has adopted a policy to fund the rapid construction of nuclear plants. As of 2022, China had fifty-one operational nuclear power plants and twenty under construction. The problem with nuclear reactors is not necessarily safety but rather that they are extremely expensive to build and take years to achieve full production. This makes it likely that China will be forced to devote significantly more resources to nuclear reactors and less to coal-fired energy in order to deal with its long-term energy demands.

All of these problems taken together, along with the addition of a binding deadline to the Paris Accord, should be more than enough to keep Xi Jinping and his colleagues awake at night as they try to balance domestic priorities and the health of the Chinese population with a rapidly deteriorating planet.

CHAPTER TEN

TOXIC AIR AND NOT ENOUGH WATER

The best man is like water. Water is good, it benefits all things and does not compete with them. It dwells in lowly places that all disdain. This is why it is so near to Tao.

—Lao Tzu (603–531 BCE)
From *The Way of Lao Tzu* (translated by Wing-Tsit Chan)

The previous chapter focused on how climate change and China's environmental policies place it in a precarious position, both from environmental and reputational standpoints. Here, the emphasis is on a related but distinct topic—the hugely negative consequences of being a major polluter.

I have firsthand experience with this. An American company once asked me to visit an area about one hundred miles west of Shanghai. The company was considering purchasing a Chinese-owned manufacturing facility near Wuxi. I visited Wuxi along with a senior executive of the company. When we arrived, we were escorted through a back entrance into the plant because local residents were staging a noisy protest out front. As we were touring the plant, I noticed a brilliant blue, flowing stream and said, "That's fantastic, you have such clear water." Later, I discovered that the water was essentially bleached blue because the factory was using benzene, a carcinogenic substance, and dumping the unused benzene into the stream that flowed toward Shanghai. It turned out that the protest outside consisted of local residents expressing their outrage about the company knowingly poisoning their water supply. My client did not purchase the facility.

Air and water are essential to sustain life. Of the two, air always seems to receive greater public and media attention. Wildfires, chemical leaks, factory and motor vehicle emissions, and nuclear explosions visually captivate the attention of the global media as governmental bodies are called to account and pressured to provide answers.

TOXIC AIR

Few people are unaware that China has suffered from dangerously high levels of air pollution for more than forty years. Increasing levels in airborne toxins are the direct result of China's decades-long rapid industrialization as its leadership went all in to claim the title of world's largest manufacturing center. Beginning in the mid-1980s in the southern region of China known as the Pearl River Delta, explosive growth in industrialization began and then spread throughout the rest of the country, particularly along the coastal areas. Special economic zones provided by provincial governments became homes to hundreds of thousands of factories feeding China's growing export markets. The long-term impact of fast and nonregulated industrialization is that China's air quality continues to worsen.

In recent years, dangerously high levels of air pollution have become so concerning that a number of foreign embassies located in Beijing host limited personnel, and in some cases have discouraged family members from residing in Beijing, citing the health risks air pollution can pose, particularly to young children. It is widely known that the U.S. embassy constantly monitors air quality in Beijing as well as at its five consulates spread throughout China. One particular fact often cited is how Beijing's industries lead the world in highly toxic mercury emissions. Even worse, industry-generated air pollution is exacerbated by emissions from motor vehicles in China powered by gasoline and diesel fuels. While China is beginning a major shift in production toward electric vehicles, toxic emissions will continue.

Without a doubt, air pollution is a critical concern facing Chinese authorities, but an even more serious threat to China's economic viability involves the other necessary life element—water.

WATER

At the 73rd Academy Awards, Julia Roberts won the Oscar for Best Actress as the titular character in the 2000 film *Erin Brockovich*. The film was based on a true story: Erin Brockovich was a legal assistant in the early 1990s who accidentally stumbled across documents indicating a massive corporate cover-up. An alarming number of citizens in Hinkley, California, had developed tumors and Hodgkin's lymphoma, and the utility company Pacific Gas & Electric (PG&E) was, for reasons not then publicly revealed, purchasing their homes and covering their medical bills. As the story develops, it becomes clear that the groundwater around Hinkley was polluted with hexavalent chromium, a deadly carcinogen. Eventually this led to the filing of a class action lawsuit in which more than 600 individual plaintiffs sued PG&E, alleging that the company had knowingly been contaminating the groundwater in Hinckley for decades. PG&E was ultimately found liable and ordered to pay $333 million to the plaintiffs. While the movie was a Hollywood version of the story, the fact that it actually happened and tragically affected so many lives exposed how something as basic and taken for granted as water, if contaminated, can have devastating long-term implications.

WATER POLLUTION. According to publicly available sources, up to one half of China's population in 2024 is unable to access safe drinking water without it first being treated. Whether this figure is totally accurate, no one really knows. However, the situation is measurably worse in rural areas; at least two-thirds of China's rural population (about 674 million people) relies on tainted water to get through their daily lives. That rural China is at such a high risk should come as no real surprise. Chemicals used to boost agricultural production in rural areas inevitably lead to runoff, which pollutes the surrounding surface and groundwater. Then, along China's coastlines where about two-thirds of the Chinese population lives, wastewater is often either improperly treated or not treated at all. The insidious reality about consuming polluted water is that it can take years or even decades to produce palpable health issues. Because the effects do not present themselves immediately (unlike an air quality alert), water pollution in China unfortunately is viewed as a less urgent problem.[1]

WATER SHORTAGES. In addition to polluted water and the health dangers it presents, China faces another equally serious threat. China is now experiencing critical shortages of water. This was never more apparent than in the summer of 2022, when soaring temperatures enveloped much of China. According to experts, it was the worst heat wave since the 1960s. In parts of Central and Southwestern China, recorded temperatures reached 110 degrees Fahrenheit. In addition to the heat, rainfall was at an all-time low. This drastically suppressed water levels in parts of the Yangtze River from which hydropower is generated, and farmers depend on water for their crops. As hydropower generation plummeted, factories in Southern China's Sichuan Province (about twenty cities) were ordered to scale back production (including the Foxconn Technology Group, which is a major supplier to Apple Inc.). This situation dealt economic blows to both manufacturing and agricultural sectors in China.

Consider how this is a truly serious MaxTrend® confronting Chinese officials. Since the northern part of China is a historically dry area lacking widespread rainfall, Southern China has been viewed as having abundant water resources friendly to agriculture. Unfortunately, this wide availability of water was taken for granted for decades. Things changed drastically in the 1980s when China undertook its massive industrialization initiatives.

Most people think of Beijing, Shanghai, Chengdu, Guangzhou, and Hong Kong as China's key economic, governmental, and business centers because they are the most familiar. In reality, China has more than 160 cities with a population of more than one million residents. Consider, for example, the Chinese city of Shenzhen. While Shenzhen has been inhabited for more than one thousand years, it began as a small border city midway between Mainland China and Hong Kong SAR when Hong Kong was under British control. In 1979, Shenzhen had between 30,000 and 40,000 inhabitants (no one is sure of the exact number). Then, when one of the first special economic zones was set up by the Chinese government in the early 1980s, Shenzhen became a magnet for foreign investment, as it is in the heart of the Pearl River Delta and near Guangzhou (formerly Canton). The first time I visited Shenzhen was in 1985, when it was still a small city of less than 100,000 people. I remember taking the hour-long train ride from Hong Kong through what was then called the "New Territories" and finally reaching the Lo Wu Railway Station. Disembarking from the train, I walked across a narrow bridge over a fetid river and laid my eyes on Shenzhen, which was just beginning to undergo its massive expansion. That Shenzhen no longer exists. Shenzhen has experienced unbelievable industrialization since the mid-1980s, at one point being tagged with the honor of being the fastest-growing city in the history of the world. No one knows the actual population of today's Shenzhen. Officially it is listed as China's sixth largest city with a population of 12.36 million inhabitants, but if you examine the metro-area data, actual numbers may approach 20 million.

With all of its commercial successes, one major problem experienced by Shenzhen is that it doesn't have adequate sources of water. Shenzhen is a city falling short of providing enough potable water to serve its population, and the situation is getting worse. And Shenzhen is not alone. The same massive growth has occurred in lesser-known cities all over China since the early 1980s, and the pressures of having enough potable water are multiplied over and over again.

Because of ongoing water shortages, China is permanently losing irrigable land at a rapid pace. China now finds itself the largest importer of agricultural goods on the planet. This is forcing the Chinese government to seek out ways to generate, or at least redirect, sources of water to these areas, with both good and bad results. One impact has been on the dams on the Mekong River. China has built eleven hydropower dams upstream, which has interfered with vast quantities of water that would otherwise naturally flow to countries south of China such as Thailand, Laos, Myanmar, Vietnam, and Cambodia.[2] Because there is no easy answer to the widespread water shortages throughout China, this will remain a critical challenge facing the country's leadership for decades to come. There is no quick fix, and if unchecked, water pollution and shortages will remain serious problems.

CHAPTER ELEVEN

THE CORROSIVE EFFECTS OF CORRUPTION

Corruption is a huge hurdle for any country aspiring to be a world leader, but this is particularly true for China. The existence of corruption discourages other countries from doing business with China and fosters inefficiencies as well as low morale. By its nature, corruption inevitably weakens a strong country. To his credit, Xi Jinping recognizes this and has made real attempts to address and eliminate corruption in China. Xi's decade-long anticorruption campaign has also served as a way to clamp down on private companies considered to be too powerful by China's central government. China has a long tradition of corruption that's difficult to overcome because it has a huge number of low-paid government officials who are all too eager to accept a bribe to offset their subpar wages. There's a concept in China—guanxi—that loosely translates to "connections" and connotes that exchanging favors for money or other gifts is proper and justified. Xi's efforts to clean up corruption have been hampered by this long-standing tradition.

This MaxTrend® is about the role corruption plays in the global economy. While the focus of this book is China, corruption, whether private, commercial, or governmental, is universal. No country, including the United States, is immune. Central to most forms of corruption are the big three—politics, power, and money.

Early in my career, I worked in the U.S. Senate as a legislative counsel. Part of my job was to meet with lobbyists who were seeking support for pieces of legislation they were paid to promote. One particular lobbyist who represented a sports league then in its infancy was particularly memorable. This lobbyist was seeking support for a bill that would grant certain antitrust exemptions to his league similar to the antitrust exemptions that had previously been granted by Congress to professional baseball and football. His practiced technique was to open with: "Let me have just ten minutes of your time, and I'll tell you exactly what the senator should consider." True to his word, his pitch always took less than ten minutes, but on occasion we would end up talking about other issues. I remember one conversation in which the lobbyist candidly offered his personal views of politicians, saying they usually fell into three categories. To paraphrase what I remember him saying: "There are many politicians who are simply in it for the prestige. They love to be called Congressman-this or Senator-that and to sit at the Kennedy Center and prize the prestige it brings in a city where everyone knows their name. Then there is the second type: the politicians who are in it for the money. Those politicians use their office as a platform to accumulate wealth for themselves, family, and friends. Then there is a third category—those are the politicians who are in it for the power." From his perspective, the smallest percentage of politicians fall into the third category, yet they have the potential to either create the greatest good or cause the most harm. Because they are not driven by money or ego, they are singularly focused on what they can accomplish. Switching this theory to China, Chinese Communist Party members with low-level party roles play the game for the money or social benefits. Most high-ranking CCP officials are in it for the power.

XI TARGETS CORRUPTION

While corruption exists in every country around the world, China, an ancient and proud culture with roots dating back more than four thousand years, operates under its own unique forms of power dynamics and influence peddling. Those who have visited or spent time seriously studying China are familiar with the Chinese concept of *guanxi*.

Guanxi essentially means "connections." *Guanxi* begins with one's family and closest personal friends and, like rings on a tree, moves outward. *Guanxi* means you can access the ability and the power to benefit others in exchange for money, friendship, or self-advancement.

Since 2013, Xi Jinping has insisted that the CCP continually and aggressively implement China's comprehensive anticorruption campaign as a key policy initiative. But in a country like China that is totally controlled by one governing party, corralling corruption is likely to most affect those who have the least. In 2020, Premier Li Keqiang stated that more than 600 million people in China had a monthly income of 1,000 yuan (US$157). This is significant. While China does have 400 million middle-income residents, much of the Chinese population earns less than US$2,500 per year. It is those individuals with little to lose who are most prone to accepting bribes and participating in corrupt activities for personal financial gain, and they will continue doing so.

Xi Jinping represents the fifth generation of Chinese leadership since the CCP came to power in 1949. Of course, each of his predecessors at one time or another expressed a desire to combat corruption, but none made it a real priority. But Xi Jinping did. When Xi assumed leadership in 2013, he immediately embraced as his personal commitment the need to fight corruption within China. No one else at the time knew the inner workings of China better than Xi Jinping, who had managed to rise from a childhood of forced labor on a rural farm to the premier height of Chinese politics. Xi clearly recognized that corruption would seriously hinder China's ability to evolve into a world leader. While some individuals may have doubted him then, they don't anymore. Xi was serious and driven.

In China, the word "corruption" is rarely spoken aloud. What you hear more often is that someone was punished for "violating Communist Party discipline and laws." This is the case because the approximately 98 million members of the CCP influence and ultimately control all decisions affecting the entirety of Chinese society. Therefore, the Western concept of governmental corruption (i.e., illegally paying a public official money to do something) does not necessarily pertain to China. Sometimes, instead of corruption, *guanxi* comes into play.

Xi Jinping has attacked corruption on two levels. First, investigations have been carried out by the National Supervisory Commission, which acts as China's watchdog for uncovering improper activities within the government. At first, Xi's anticorruption campaign focused on corrupt activities carried out by lower-level public officials. Like in many societies, particularly in poorer countries throughout the developing world, Chinese government officials were traditionally paid very little. Therefore it was normal and expected practice that lower-level officials possessing the power to grant or refuse certain government approvals could be influenced to act favorably in exchange for offers of paid vacations, fancy meals, or other minor incentives. When this kind of activity becomes widespread and expected in any society, the economy as a whole will ultimately suffer because, by its nature, bribery is not efficient. This should be a genuine concern for leaders like Xi.

Lower-level Chinese officials (unfortunately often referred to as "flies") were an obvious target for Xi's early anticorruption initiatives. Depending on the severity of their actions, those individuals could be disciplined, expelled from the CCP, or on rare occasions face criminal charges. However, Xi did not just focus on the "flies." Soon the conduct of increasingly wealthy Chinese tycoons in the private sector—better known as "big tigers"—came under his review. In 2018, Xi's anticorruption campaign adopted a new slogan: "*Saohei chúe.*" In English, this slogan basically translates to "Sweep away black and eliminate evil." According to published statistics, between 2018 and the end of 2021, over 650,000 CCP and government officials were punished in some manner, and some private companies and individuals found themselves charged with criminal activities. Also according to a published report by the Communist Party Central Commission for Discipline Inspection and the National Supervisory Commission, in 2021 627,000 officials were charged with violating CCP laws. Of the 627,000, about two-thirds were lower-level officials.

CORRUPTION IN CHINA'S PRIVATE SECTOR

Following the years when Xi Jinping primarily focused on rooting out corruption within the CCP, he turned his attention to profitable Chinese entities that were seen as potential counterweights to the power of the CCP. At the party's Sixth Plenum in 2021, Xi promoted his anticorruption drive in equal importance with other top goals of the CCP such as alleviating poverty, encouraging development, and strengthening CCP governance. This was a lead-up to the October 2022 meeting at which Xi's term as China's premier leader was extended indefinitely (something that was unprecedented since Mao's death in 1976).

There have been public reports of investigations initiated by CCP officials into large and powerful Chinese companies such as Alibaba Group, WeChat, Tencent Holdings Ltd., and others. One of the most extreme examples was the case against Lai Xiaomin, who served as a chairman of Huarong Asset Management. At one time, Huarong was one of China's largest state-controlled management asset firms. Lai received a death sentence for allegedly taking massive bribes and was executed in January 2021. This was a loud and clear message that those who could be prosecuted for corruption would range from the underlings all the way to the top. Other investigations have focused on members of China's judicial system. Unlike the West, where judges spend years as practicing attorneys before being appointed to the bench, judges in China assume their judicial positions very early in their careers. According to the *South China Morning Post* (September 2021), nearly one-third of former Chinese judges who continued to practice law after leaving the bench violated rules on conflicts of interest. Under

Chinese law, a retiring judge, while able to continue practicing law, is not allowed to represent clients in court for two years, and there is a lifetime ban on handling cases that came before them formally.

The challenge Xi Jinping will continue to face is to balance the cultural tradition regarding the use of *guanxi* with anticorruption investigations, increased governance on point, and consistent administration of the law. Failing to get a handle on this MaxTrend® will set back Xi's ambitions for China.

CHAPTER TWELVE

WHAT'S FUELING THE GLOBAL ARMS RACE?

The signs are everywhere—the world is engaged in an ever-accelerating arms race. The total amount of global spending on weapons and military equipment is shocking. According to the Stockholm International Peace Research Institute (SIPRI), world military expenditures have now passed the US$2 trillion mark. The arms race is more than just an accounting of how many ships, planes, missiles, uniformed personnel, and, in some cases, nuclear weapons a country possesses now versus a decade ago. Predicting military growth is more complex than merely calculating what percentage of a country's gross domestic product is devoted to weapons expenditures. What drives the level of investment in military capabilities is how countries assess their internal security needs balanced with the possibility of external threats. Then, is a country maintaining its military in a primarily defensive posture, or is its military designed to be an offensive force?

No country in the history of the world has ever felt truly secure unless it was maintaining a credible military capability. China is no different. Xi Jinping as the ultimate and unchallenged head of the Chinese military has decided to transform China into a military colossus. Over the last twenty-seven years, the amount China spends on its military has markedly increased. Beyond just ramping up the number of attack planes, ballistic missiles, naval craft, submarines, nuclear weapons, and land-based capabilities, China has funded its military so it can project both an offensive and defensive military posture. Central to this military buildup is China's desire to exert unchallenged control over the South China Sea, including the ability to exploit its vast oil and natural gas reserves. China has also devoted enormous sums in order to strengthen its capabilities on both land and sea in anticipation of imposing its goal of reunification with Taiwan.

CHINA'S BLUE-WATER AMBITIONS

When the Soviet Union collapsed in the early 1990s, China was a surprising beneficiary. Until then, China felt forced to station a large percentage of its People's Liberation Army (PLA) throughout the region to defend itself against possible land-based threats from its largest neighbors, Russia and India. With the Soviet Union no longer a perceived threat, funding was freed up for expanding China's military. This led to a massive restructuring of the PLA with the goal of transforming China's military from a primarily defensive force into a global offensive power. Freed from land-based threats, China focused its efforts on an expansion of the People's Liberation Army Navy (PLAN). Prior to that point, the PLAN basically had acted as a kind of coast guard primarily responsible for policing China's inland waterways and coastal hot spots.

Chinese officials correctly assessed that Japan and Korea posed no present or future military threat to China, nor did Taiwan. Likewise, the countries bordering on the South China Sea (Malaysia, Vietnam, Brunei, the Philippines, and a handful of others) never constituted any strategic threat to China's sovereignty as long as free passage through the strategic South China Sea lanes for exporting goods was uninterrupted. With no surrounding nations posing a threat to the Chinese coastline, the PLAN was able to evolve beyond a purely defensive structure. Like a baseball player at the plate with three balls and no strikes, swinging hard posed no risk, so China invested heavily in the PLAN. It was obvious to any serious observer that China was pursuing a "blue water" strategy.[1]

The desire to pursue a blue-water strategy was triggered by the region nearest and dearest to the Chinese—the South China Sea. This is a tactical area for China because most of what is manufactured on the Chinese Mainland and destined for export by maritime ships travels through the South China Sea, primarily heading to Japanese and American markets or toward Africa and Europe.

Located close to China's coastline, in the Yellow Sea, the East China Sea, and the South China Sea, the first chain of islands essentially stretches from the southernmost Chinese islands to north of Japan and Korea. This geographic area holds an extremely high strategic interest for the Chinese. There is a second island chain farther removed from China's shores that embraces all of the waters within the first chain as well as the Philippine Sea that lies between the Philippines and Guam.

Two reasons explain why China is so intent on asserting its sovereignty over the South China Sea and beyond. First, China has long resented the presence of the U.S. Navy throughout the Indo-Pacific region. For six decades following the end of World War II, only one blue-water navy ruled the world's oceans, and that was the U.S. Navy. The transparent mission of the U.S. Navy has always been to guarantee that the South China Sea and surrounding areas remain open for free passage of goods headed both to and from the region. China, though, embraces a darker view of the U.S. Navy's presence in the region. China believes that the U.S. Navy exists to blockade Chinese ports if a conflict were to arise between China and the United States. While the prospect of such a blockade is extremely remote, it served as justification for Chinese leaders (and particularly Xi Jinping) to upgrade the PLAN's capabilities. How was this possible? For one thing, 40 percent of global shipbuilding capacity is based in China. Since these shipbuilding activities are carried out by Chinese state-owned enterprises (SOEs), it has been possible, if ordered by the Chinese government, for those shipbuilders to quickly shift the configuration of ships being constructed from commercial to military.

There is an equally important second reason why the Chinese are aggressively asserting dominance over the South China Sea, and that reason is economic. Massive untapped reserves of natural gas and petroleum lie beneath the South China Sea, and China sees these reserves as absolutely essential to its continued economic growth. Any break in China's importation of oil and petroleum products from the Middle East (including Iran) would significantly disrupt Chinese manufacturing capabilities. This is one reason why China consumes increasing amounts of petroleum from Russia.

Now that China has achieved its status as a leading global economic power, it is moving forward to establish its own blue-water navy. While today the United States has the world's only true blue-water navy, the Chinese are spending vast sums to catch up. The U.S. Department of Defense published a public document titled *2020 China Military Power Report.* The report confirmed that China can claim to have the "world's largest navy" as determined by number of ships, including formidable naval vessels such as aircraft carriers, one cruiser, destroyers, frigates, and other surface vessels, as well as fifty-two submarines (six of which are nuclear-powered). Because of the current size of its navy, China is now the only possible challenger to the long-standing status of the United States as the leading military power in the Western Pacific. The U.S. Navy maintains a force of about 293 ships, but it is important to understand that numbers of ships do not tell the entire story, because when measured by total tonnage, the U.S. Navy fleet is larger and more technologically complex than China's. To be precise, the U.S. Navy has eleven aircraft carriers, all of which are nuclear-powered, as well as sixty-nine submarines, all of which are nuclear, and nine more have been recently authorized by Congress. The U.S. Navy, with its 333,000 personnel, exceeds the size of the PLAN by about 80,000. When it comes to sophisticated electronic warfare, the U.S. Navy has a clear lead, but the Chinese are working hard to close the gap.

AN INCREASINGLY TENSE SITUATION

While China prefers to describe its military as "defensive" in nature, China has the second largest military budget in the world (after the United States). Considering the massive resources being devoted by Chinese leadership to expanding the size of the PLAN, China clearly hopes to eventually displace the role that the U.S. Navy has played throughout the Pacific since the end of World War II. As an important first step, the Chinese have erected sophisticated military bases on three island chains in the South China Sea. By openly declaring sovereignty over the Spratly Islands and other maritime atolls, the Chinese can close off the South China Sea if they so desire. The only counterforce capable of blocking this is the U.S. Pacific Fleet. It is obvious why nations worldwide are increasingly concerned about the aggressive nature of China's presence. It is now a common occurrence for U.S. reconnaissance planes flying over international waters of the South China Sea to be harassed by Chinese military aircraft and warned not to enter what China claims as its airspace.

Even though China's PLAN is the second most powerful navy in the world today, the Chinese continue to add to its capabilities. China ultimately targets all of the Western Pacific as its sovereign domain, and this worries nations throughout the region that are dependent on free transit throughout the world's oceans and strategic trade routes. The biggest concern for Western powers is what will happen if China decides to unilaterally take aggressive action against Taiwan. The truth is, an increasingly powerful PLAN makes it logistically difficult for the U.S. Navy to repulse an outright invasion. The back-and-forth encounters between China and the United States are played out on the world's waters every day.

THE MAD STRATEGY

If you are an American sixty years old or older, you and I probably share a common memory from our childhoods—though nightmare might be a better description. During the 1950s, 1960s, and even into the 1970s, the threat of a nuclear war breaking out between the United States and the USSR was an ever-present reality. I will never forget, as an elementary school student, being directed by my teachers to "duck and cover" under my desk in the event of a nuclear attack. Students were told that we would be safe crouching under our small wood desks if the Russians were to attack suddenly and there were no time to reach a bomb shelter. Of course, huddling under school desks would never actually have protected us, but I realize now that this charade was the only thing the grown-ups could think of to make us less afraid.

During the Cold War (1949–1991), the U.S. military erected Nike missile bases around major U.S. cities that were intended to intercept inbound Soviet nuclear missiles. Offensively, the United States maintained a massive fleet of B-52 bombers capable of carrying nuclear weapons 24/7. There was even a top-secret underground bunker constructed in what is today's Greenbrier Resort located in White Sulphur Springs, West Virginia. Dug deep into the Allegheny Mountains is a massive emergency fallout shelter built at the height of the Cold War and intended to protect members of the U.S. Congress in the event of a nuclear attack, real or threatened. In theory, if Washington DC fell under attack by Soviet missiles, the entire U.S. Congress and top staff members could be quickly whisked off to the West Virginia bunker behind a twenty-five-ton blast door.[2] Then there was the Cuban Missile Crisis, when for twelve days in 1962 the United States and the Soviet Union came terrifyingly close to the edge of thermonuclear war. Had President John F. Kennedy not ignored the advice of his generals at the time, who knows what might have happened. The Cold War between the United States and the USSR continued unabated until the collapse of the Soviet Union in December 1991.

In the course of this unsettling and escalating arms race, the doctrine of MAD—Mutual Assured Destruction—was conceived. MAD was a strategy of nuclear deterrence that experts used to convince the public that a nuclear war would never actually occur, because if the United States and the USSR unleashed nuclear missiles on each other, both countries would be destroyed. Following the collapse of the Soviet Union, public concern about the prospects of nuclear war diminished for a time, but that concern slowly began ramping up again for a variety of reasons, the most obvious being North Korea aggressively expanding its nuclear weapons capacity (including intercontinental ballistic missiles [ICBMs]). Other points of concern are Pakistan building up its own nuclear weapons to protect itself against perceived threats from India, and, of course, Iran's nuclear ambitions, triggering continued worries in Israel and throughout the Middle East.

CHINA JOINS THE NUCLEAR RACE

Until the ascendancy of Xi Jinping in 2013, China was slow in coming to the nuclear party. Even though China detonated its first nuclear weapon in 1964, its nuclear arsenal grew at a relatively slow pace. That has all changed. China's effort to build up its military capacity, particularly in the nuclear area, has been underway for over a decade.

According to publicly available statistics, Russia currently maintains an arsenal of 5,899 nuclear weapons, and the United States has 5,244. While China comes in a distant third, it reportedly possesses about 410 deliverable nuclear weapons, with more on the way. In addition, China claims it has more than 140 functional ICBMs. What has become increasingly clear is that China under Xi Jinping has deliberately accelerated its efforts to develop a formidable nuclear capacity. According to a 2021 U.S. congressional report, the U.S. Department of Defense predicts that by the year

2030, China will possess up to one thousand nuclear warheads. This is a serious concern for many nations, and particularly for the United States.

When pressed, the Chinese describe their current nuclear policy in three parts. Part One is China's promise of "no first use." In short, China says it will only *respond* to what would appear to be a nuclear attack. Part Two is China's plan to maintain its nuclear force in a "moderate state of alert." Part Three states that in the event China is directly attacked, it will be prepared to "mount a resolute counterattack" against any and all of its perceived enemies. Putting all three parts together, China's nuclear policy is not a simple "sit-back-and-wait" scenario. Once again, if projections are correct, China intends to expand its nuclear capacity to one thousand nuclear warheads over the next seven to ten years. Even then, China still will be in third place as to the number of nuclear weapons, though still far ahead of other countries possessing nuclear weapons. This is in comparison to the United Kingdom, which maintains 225 nuclear weapons, France with 290, India with 156, and Pakistan with 165. While it is no secret that Israel also possesses nuclear weapons, there are no public sources to document how many actually exist or can be effectively delivered in the event of war involving Israel.

WHY DOES CHINA CARE?

All of this begs the question, why does China feel it needs to maintain such a large nuclear capacity? Clearly Russia poses no nuclear threat to China, and neither do other countries in Asia (including India and Pakistan), so why is China so concerned? While there have been past border disputes, including relatively recently between India and China, those disputes have never reached a point where nuclear retaliation would be a possibility.

So if not Russia, India, or Pakistan, what is it that has China on edge? Some believe the heightened political tensions in recent years between China and the United States suggest that China feels it must possess a large nuclear inventory in the event of a first strike by the U.S. However, unless China intends to initiate unprovoked aggression against any of its neighbors in Southeast Asia or the Philippines, Japan, Korea, or, more likely, Taiwan, an oversized nuclear force for China makes no sense. It is Taiwan that continues to be a constant irritant for Xi Jinping and China's military. The Chinese government has unequivocally declared that Taiwan is not an independent country but is in fact part of the People's Republic of China. It will be interesting to see over the long run whether Putin's invasion of Ukraine dampens or encourages China's efforts to extend sovereignty over Taiwan. In the event of a military invasion, it appears likely the United States will feel obligated to defend Taiwan, though formal U.S. government policies as to the status of Taiwan remain deliberately ambiguous.

Under Xi Jinping, China over the next decade will continue its efforts to modernize and expand its nuclear capabilities, including constructing land-, sea-, and air-based delivery platforms. As publicly disclosed by the U.S. Department of Defense, the Chinese military is constructing numerous missile silos in locations throughout Western China, any of which have the ability to strike the United States.

Unfortunately, it appears probable that a situation similar to the decades-long Cold War between the USSR and the United States will resurface in Asia because of China's rapid and ongoing efforts at nuclear expansion. China's tripling its nuclear arsenal over the next few years will create pressure on countries such as India to increase their own nuclear capacities. At the end of the day, Xi Jinping's ultimate goal regarding nuclear capabilities is twofold. By the year 2049—the one hundredth anniversary of the Chinese Communist Party—China desires both a military and economic presence equal to or greater than what the United States then possesses. China views the Pacific region and Asia as its sphere of influence and is likely to do whatever it takes to push that agenda. Because of this, Japan, which has maintained a strong antinuclear policy since the end of World War II, will feel forced to reevaluate whether it needs to develop its own nuclear force. Similar questions will be raised by leadership in South Korea due to its proximity to China.

I have no doubt China's increasingly aggressive and expensive efforts to build up its nuclear capacity will accelerate America's efforts already underway to modernize its own nuclear arsenal. Where this all ends is unknown, but the historical concept of MAD as a guarantee that there will never be a nuclear confrontation is far less comforting today than it was in times past.

REACTIONS TO A MILITARIZED CHINA

At the heart of China's efforts to control the South China Sea are its "nine-dash line" claims.[3] This refers to China's argument that it has legitimate claims to sovereignty over the South China Sea because this is where China's borders were "historically" located. The nine-dash line is the basis on which China asserts rights over the Spratly,[4] Paracel, and Pratas Islands in the South China Sea.

China is paying and will continue to pay a price for its rapid military buildup as other nations respond. Each of its five nearest neighbors—Vietnam, Malaysia, Indonesia, the Philippines, and Taiwan—is already reacting in one way or another.

VIETNAM. Vietnam has found itself engaged in territorial disputes with China for literally decades. Because Vietnam shares the largest coastline along the South China Sea with China, it has found itself drawn into contests with China over which country can legitimately claim mineral, fishing, and trading route rights to the South China Sea. The South China Sea represents both a strategic waterway vital to trade as well as a basin containing massive reserves of unexploited oil and natural gas. As far back as 1974, China and Vietnam clashed over their claims to the Paracel Islands. Fourteen years later, China and Vietnam again came to blows over which nation had legitimate rights and sovereignty over the Spratly Islands. That dispute received international attention when seventy-four Vietnamese fishermen and soldiers were killed and three ships were lost as the two countries battled over rights to the far-flung atolls and reefs. Over the years since, violent and nonviolent confrontations have occurred involving Vietnamese and Chinese fishermen. One example was the attempt by the National Petroleum Corporation of China to claim the South China Sea's natural reserves by erecting a platform for the extraction of gas and oil. The platform was located in an area over which Vietnam claimed sovereignty as its "exclusive economic zone" (EEZ). Another complication for Vietnam is posed by its historically close ties with Russia (as the counterweight to Chinese expansionism in the region). This has spurred the Vietnamese to continue modernizing their military, particularly in the naval domain. Because Vietnam has no serious conflicts with any of its closest Southeast Asian neighbors, its buildup of weapons is to counteract threats—real or perceived—from China.

MALAYSIA. The nine-dash-line claim directly impacts how Malaysia views China. Because Malaysia, like most other nations in the region, has adopted the United Nations Convention on the Law of the Sea (UNCLOS), Malaysia argues that it has the legal right to claim up to 200 miles from its borders as its EEZ. As the Malaysians have had fewer disputes with the Chinese than the Vietnamese, as of now Malaysia has only moderately increased its military capacities. There has been no increase in Malaysian naval expenditures in recent years, which would certainly be viewed by China as a threat.

INDONESIA. Even more vocal than the Malaysians, the Indonesians have rejected China's claims under its nine-dash line to occupy the 200 nautical miles claimed by Indonesia as its EEZ. Indonesia has aggressively tried to enforce its EEZ rights against both China and nearby Vietnam. While military spending in Indonesia has remained relatively constant under President Widodo, Indonesia objects to Chinese incursions into the Natuna Island region, which lies within 200 nautical miles of Indonesia. Chinese ships from time to time sail there. Despite this, it is unlikely that Indonesia's purchases of modern weapons from the United States, Russia, or South Korea are a cause for concern for China. Like Malaysia, Indonesia, while outwardly opposing China's expansive policy throughout the South China Sea, is unwilling to directly confront the Chinese and thus increase tensions. China cannot realistically claim that Indonesia at this time poses any military threat to China's ongoing steps to assert sovereignty over most of the South China Sea.

THE PHILIPPINES. Other than Taiwan, no country has engaged in more confrontations with China in the South China Sea than the Philippines. Since the history of conflicts between these two countries appears elsewhere in this book, what follows is a brief synopsis. The United Nations–sponsored treaty UNCLOS came into effect in 1982 and was ratified by the Philippines in 1984. The appeal of UNCLOS to the Philippines was that the Philippines could claim itself as an "archipelago state." Being recognized as an archipelago state under UNCLOS, the Philippines could claim an EEZ of 200 nautical miles around each of its islands. As a result, the Philippines asserted sovereignty over the highly disputed Spratly Islands as well as the reefs surrounding it known as the Scarborough Shoal. After years of clashing with China, the Philippines decided to file a formal claim against China in an international arbitration proceeding. Specifically, the Philippines challenged China's nine-dash-line claims and China's efforts to exploit natural resources within the claimed Philippines EEZ. In a formal proceeding filed in the Permanent Court of Arbitration, after hearing the arguments, the tribunal ruled in favor of the Philippines, rejecting China's nine-dash-line claims. Almost immediately, the Chinese rejected the decision of the arbitrators, and

China continued to pursue its efforts to expand its influence through-out the South China Sea. When Philippines president Rodrigo Roa Duterte took power in 2016, he did not directly pressure the Chinese to honor the arbitration decision. This encouraged China to continue expanding its presence and activities in the South China Sea. Because the Philippine military does not represent a major counterweight to China in the region, the Chinese cannot legitimately claim that their military buildup is a reaction to a Philippine threat. Since Duterte has been replaced by President Ferdinand "Bongbong" Marcos Jr., the relationship between China and the Philippines has grown increasingly tense over disputes in the South China Sea.

TAIWAN. The subject of Taiwan and China is covered extensively elsewhere in this book, so I will not repeat that analysis here except to restate that while Taiwan, unlike other countries in the region, does maintain a significant military capability with modernized weapons systems, it is no real threat to China. Taiwan simply wants to be left alone. China's persistent efforts to "encourage" (force) reunification with Taiwan are more than a matter of national pride; they reflect an avowed goal of Xi Jinping.

In a nutshell, China's widespread and aggressive expansion into the South China Sea based on its nine-dash-line theory seems to have succeeded, at least for now. While five nations—Vietnam, Malaysia, Indonesia, the Philippines, and Taiwan—have had their EEZs impinged upon by the Chinese, none (except for Taiwan) has directly responded with a significant buildup of its military capacities. One can only assume that while these nations may have legitimate claims (and in the case of the Philippines, an international arbitration judgment), they have decided not to escalate those claims in such a way as to give China a reason to retaliate.

However, Southeast Asia is not the only region closely monitoring China's global military buildup. India, Japan, and South Korea are all weighing the risks of a militarized China.

INDIA. With a population of 1.43 billion people, India is not directly influenced by the actions of the Chinese in the South China Sea unless its trade routes are disrupted. Since becoming a sovereign country in January 1950, India has maintained a robust military infrastructure—the Indian Army, the Indian Air Force, and the Indian Navy—with the world's largest volunteer army and second largest military force by number. India without a doubt is a key power in the Indian Ocean region, which extends as far as Africa to the west and the Malacca Straits to the east.[5] Because India has a sizable nuclear arsenal and shares borders with China (some of which remain in dispute) and Pakistan, India's commitment to maintaining a strong military should not be underestimated. China has historically viewed India as a potential rival, particularly when border disputes have escalated to direct conflicts. India's annual defense expenditures are about US$71 billion, which makes Indian military spending the third largest in the world after the United States and China. Under Prime Minister Shri Narendra Modi, India has begun to overhaul its current military structure, which is likely to lead it to closer ties with the United States and its allies.

SOUTH KOREA. Another major player in the region is South Korea (the Republic of Korea). South Korea currently has a formidable military capability, and some experts rank South Korea as the world's sixth most powerful military. With a population of nearly 52 million, South Korea has between 500,000 and 555,000 active military personnel and spends about US$50 billion per year on its defense budget. South Korea has an outsized military in light of its size, with about 1,600 total aircraft, 25 percent of which are either interceptors or fighters. It also has twelve destroyers, eighteen frigates, eleven corvettes, and twenty-two submarines. While South Korea does not have its own aircraft carriers, it does have two helicopter carriers. South Korea has little choice but to maintain such a high-level military capability because of North Korea. North Korea (the Democratic People's Republic of Korea) has over 1.1 million ground troops as well as nuclear warheads, ballistic missiles, and other offensive capabilities. This forced South Korea to deploy much of its military capability up and around the 38th parallel. A major strategic ally for the Korean military is the United States. About 28,500 U.S. Army, Navy, and Air Force troops are permanently located in South Korea. Spending about 3 percent of its GDP on military expenditures makes South Korea, on a percentage basis, one of the top militarized countries in the world. Nevertheless, South Korea faces long-term demographic problems. With an extremely low birth rate, it has trouble maintaining the size and quality of its military. While South Korea does mandate military service for all Korean men between the ages of eighteen and thirty-five,[6] it is becoming increasingly difficult to maintain a sufficient number of trained troops to act as a deterrent to North Korea. Thus, while the South Korean military is modern, engaged, and sophisticated, it in no way presents any kind of threat to the Chinese.

JAPAN. That brings us to Japan. For the first half of the 20th century, Japan was the scourge of Asia. Occupying what is today's Korea, Japan invaded Manchuria, had a significant presence in much of China, and extended its Imperial Navy as far as East Asia. It was only with its defeat at the end of World War II that Japan was forced to renounce its military ambitions. This met with general approval by the Japanese people, who embraced a more pacifistic view of the world. For the last two decades, Japan's military spending has been capped at around 1 percent of its GDP. However, Japan recently announced its intent to double the level of its military spending. While there are numerous reasons for this, most relate to perceived and real threats posed by

China. The first is that Japan claims control over what are known as the Senkaku Islands. Those islands are also claimed by China, which refers to them as the Diaoyu Islands. Ongoing clashes between Japanese fishing boats and Chinese armed coast guard ships continue to make this a hot point between the two countries.

China's increasing focus on Taiwan is a real concern for Japan as well as other democracies in the region, as they view the future of Taiwan as closely tied to their own national interests. In fact, Japan has certain military resources located on Yonaguni Island, which is less than one hundred miles from the coast of Taiwan. Japan believes that the fate of Taiwan is critical to its own sovereignty. Japan's current leadership is now seriously reevaluating how Japan, which in theory only has a "self-defense" military force, can be more engaged in the region.

The Trump Administration for four years backed away from America's involvement in Asia. During the Biden Administration, Japan has sought out a better relationship with the United States as well as with Australia, Britain, and other European countries. Like in South Korea, there are about fifty thousand U.S. troops permanently based in Japan. Although most are located on the southern island of Okinawa, Japan has historically relied on these troops for its own defense since the end of World War II. Even while claiming its defensive posture, Japan maintains more than nine hundred warplanes, forty-eight destroyers, and twenty submarines, as well as eight Aegis missile combat systems. In fact, the Japanese military is larger than those of France, Italy, and the United Kingdom individually.

Since the end of World War II, Japan has depended on the U.S. nuclear umbrella for protection. As China's military becomes increasingly aggressive throughout the region, Japan is likely to seriously explore the advantages of becoming a nuclear power itself. This would clearly heighten tensions with China, which are historically considerable. Some experts predict that if the Japanese government decides to amend its constitution and make nuclear weapons acquisition a priority, this could be accomplished in a very short time. As mentioned, China's expansion throughout the region beyond the South China Sea has already resulted in Japan doubling the size of its overall military budget.

AUSTRALIA. Australia, although a long way from Asia, remains an important player in the region. Australia maintains its significant and far-reaching Australian Defense Force (ADF). In March 2022, Prime Minister Scott Morrison announced that Australia planned to expand the ADF by more than 30 percent over the next eighteen years. This expansion will require a much larger military force than the current 59,000 troops and one unprecedented for Australia since the end of the Vietnam War. Despite its distance from China, Australia believes it is critical to expand its defensive capabilities. Australia's move to expand its military is a direct response to increased Chinese activities because Australia is closely tied to the South Pacific Islands and sees potential concerns over the long run. Upgrading its nuclear submarine force with American technology is the most recent example.

NATO AND EUROPE

In evaluating whether China is threatened or incentivized by the military capacities of other countries, it is a mistake to focus solely on Asia. The North Atlantic Treaty Organization (NATO) is without question the largest global military alliance in the world today. Russia's 2022 attack on Ukraine energized the NATO military alliance. Within weeks of that attack, NATO moved to augment its readiness by building up the number of response forces to well over 300,000 troops. This, according to a NATO spokesman, was the largest overhaul of collective defense and deterrents since the end of the Cold War. Since Russia's attack on Ukraine, NATO has expanded beyond its thirty members (most recently adding Finland and Sweden). NATO member nations over the years were required to pledge 2 percent of their GDPs in support of the alliance. This 2 percent, instead of being a ceiling, now looks like it will become a floor. With the increasingly close relationship that exists between China and Russia, NATO will now be forced to view China for the first time as a potential concern. This is likely to lead to higher spending among the NATO members.

Perhaps the most unexpected but significant impact of the Russian invasion of Ukraine occurred in Germany, when Chancellor Olaf Scholz announced that Germany expected to double the funding for its military. In a sense, Germany is much like Japan. Following World War II, while maintaining a national force, Germany's military was mainly defensive in nature. Following the invasion of Ukraine, Germany is poised to become the largest military force in Europe and NATO. Without a doubt, Germany's decision will further accelerate military spending throughout NATO, because Germany's rebuilding of its military is welcomed by most NATO members. After the Trump Administration for four years backed away from America's historical support for NATO, the Biden Administration reversed course and renewed America's commitment to the alliance. In any case, Germany's decision to become a larger and more effective military force will undoubtedly strengthen NATO. Even Poland, which had traditionally been concerned about a strong German military, embraced Germany's decision to expand.

BENEFITS VERSUS RISKS

China, particularly under Xi Jinping, has for decades been deliberately building up its offensive military capabilities. While there was a lot of catch-up to do so that it could feel confident in its defensive military, China's military has now reached the point where it is no longer defensive in nature. China's ongoing policy to expand its reach throughout the South China Sea and into the Pacific has raised levels of concern not just in Southeast Asia and Taiwan but also increasingly in South Korea and particularly Japan. What the Chinese have ended up doing is spurring countries like Japan, India, and the United States to expand their own military capabilities within the Pacific region.

To be frank, the Chinese already possess a large and rapidly growing offensive military. A military of this size is very expensive, not just to build up, but more importantly to maintain over the long run. As I describe throughout this book, China is spending much more than it needs to on its military. There are no obvious or likely threats to China's sovereignty, and if it does want to strengthen its economy, moderating military spending would make sense. For example, trying to resolve China's real estate crisis makes far more sense than bulking up its nuclear arsenal.

Russia's unexpected and unprovoked invasion of Ukraine placed pressure on NATO to expand as a global military alliance. The sad truth is that we are in the midst of an accelerating global arms race that shows no signs of slowing down. China's continuing aggressive pursuit of its military ambitions throughout the Pacific only leads to further expansion, thus speeding up the arms race. The question for Xi Jinping and China's leadership is whether this is all truly necessary to ensure China's goals. Do the benefits outweigh the risks? I think not.

CHAPTER THIRTEEN

THE RISE OF NATIONALISM
A Nightmare Returns

China is finding itself increasingly less attractive as a place both to do business and to source manufactured products for export markets. One reason is the resurgence of nationalism after a three-decade hiatus. This MaxTrend® of nationalism negatively impacts Xi Jinping and challenges his ambition for China to surpass the United States as the world's leading economic and military power.

Now that Xi Jinping has managed to successfully consolidate his three-legged power base, his goal is for China to retain its status as a premier manufacturing hub and to displace the United States as the world's leading economic and military power by 2049 (the one hundredth anniversary of the Chinese Communist Party's ascent to power in China). One MaxTrend® that is little appreciated but has the potential to derail Xi's ambitions is the rapid rise of nationalism around the world.

Nationalism is best understood when placed in a historical context. Xi is just the latest in a long line of leaders who have been caught up in (and sometimes brought down by) this trend. Let's examine how this historical drama has unfolded, and then, perhaps, we can understand the pitfalls that await any leader and country that become proponents of nationalism.

Many of us do not clearly understand what nation-states are or appreciate what roles they play in a global economy. Basically, a nation-state is a sovereign government that rules over a defined geographic territory. Nation-states control the borders, manage currencies, set immigration policies, and enforce laws governing their citizens. In theory, each nation-state is made up of a homogenous population that shares a common culture and goals. Perhaps the most brilliant mind of the 20th century, Albert Einstein, was a Jewish refugee who escaped Nazi Germany in 1933. As to the topic of nation-states, Einstein once remarked, "The state was made for man, not man for state." Einstein foresaw the potential of nation-states to either achieve great successes or commit unimaginable horrors (just consider Germany, Japan, and Italy during World War II).

The idea of a nation-state is nothing new. Dating back to long before the French Revolution, Europe was made up of a mishmash of independent fiefdoms and kingdoms asserting their own national priorities. They often embraced colonialism as a strategy to exploit other countries, particularly those in poor areas. Following the successful French Revolution, many of the monarchies in Europe were replaced by countries governed by the populace instead of kings or queens. What initially constituted these new countries (nation-states) were a common language, a shared culture, and often a homogenous population. Throughout the 19th century, nation-states continued to spring up in what is today's Europe. Monarchies, in most instances, became only a symbol of power, the United Kingdom being a perfect example.

Larger nation-states by their very nature are often aggressive, and this was particularly true after the end of World War I. The period between World War I and World War II was a virulent time, as Albert Einstein realized. He often described nationalism during that period as a "disease." Germany, Italy, and Japan, each with their autocratic leaders, embraced the nation-state mentality and sought to impose their cultures and racial philosophies on a world suffering from the economic depression of the 1930s. This inevitably led to global war, first in Europe and then later in the Pacific following Japan's unprovoked attack on Pearl Harbor.

As post–World War II Europe lay in ruins in 1945, the defeated nation-states that had failed to impose themselves on the European continent and Asia went into hibernation. Because Europe as well as Japan were economically destroyed, there were desperate calls for international cooperation in order to rebuild a devastated world economy. Multilateralism emerged. America's Marshall Plan was a prime example of significant funding directed on a multilateral basis.

The period following World War II took on a unique character, with the birth of many new international organizations and multilateral regimes, the most prominent being the United Nations. This was unlike the period between World War I and World War II, when similar efforts to create international cooperation failed. What came to be known as "globalization" was successful in revitalizing a desperately wounded world economy. The establishment of the European Union (EU) in 1957 was an early and highly successful example of how individual nations could come together under the banner of multilateral cooperation and thus promote globalization. Slowly, and then more rapidly during the 1960s and 1970s, the EU structure added more European countries under its umbrella. This accelerated after the final collapse of the Soviet Union in 1991, as former USSR satellite states joined as members of the EU and NATO.

But nothing good lasts forever. The EU bureaucracy in Brussels eventually began asserting greater and greater regulatory power over the diverse citizens of its member states. What had initially been thought of as a "monetary" union morphed into a more socially oriented group of nations. In response, a countermovement arose in Europe beginning in the mid-1990s, which was when the idea of globalism and multilateral organizations seemed to reach its peak. Books and magazines during the 1990s were filled with predictions that the "rise of globalism" was inevitable and that the nation-state was obsolete. Kenichi Ohmae, the UCLA professor and head of the Luskin School of Public Affairs, published a book in May 1996 that said it all in the title—*The End of the Nation State: The Rise of Regional Economies.* Professor Ohmae was not alone. Others published similar works, such as Gurutz Jáuregui Bereciartu's *Decline of the Nation-State.* Even leading international magazines such as *The Economist* published in-depth analyses declaring that the nation-state was no longer relevant. While they may have appeared right at the time, they in fact were wrong.[1]

During the later 1990s, even more obvious signs of discontent emerged throughout the European Union. A countermovement advocating nationalism (often in the form of right-wing political movements) asserted itself throughout diverse sectors of the European population, including some countries that had once been part of the former Soviet Union. Disaffected voters throughout Europe found themselves drawn to these movements because they believed they had missed out on the many benefits promised by the EU bureaucrats who had promoted an open and multilateral trade system. Those opposing internationalism believed their political representatives and the EU bureaucracy were out of touch with their needs. One policy wrought by globalization that they found particularly offensive was the freedom of travel and open immigration borders throughout the EU. Many viewed this a loss of their personal national identity, a concept at the core of nationalism. Throughout the EU, minority political parties sprang up, seeking to gain power within their national parliaments.

Over the last decade, nationalism became particularly pronounced in Hungary, Poland, Austria, and even Switzerland (which is not an EU member). Poland, prior to Russia's unprovoked 2022 invasion of Ukraine, was among several European nations that had gained significant notoriety within the European Union by focusing on internal policies and working to halt further integration. Perhaps the best-known political figure arguing in favor of nationalism is French politician Marine Le Pen, who aggressively articulated her views as she gained notoriety throughout Europe. Le Pen is the daughter of far-right nationalist Jean-Marie Le Pen, who himself was defeated in 2002 in a presidential runoff election. While Marine Le Pen was defeated in her bid to be president by Emmanuel Macron in 2017, and then again in 2022, those who embrace Le Pen's outlook remain no less vocal today.

BREXIT AND TRUMP

Without a doubt, the best-known example of renewed nationalism revealed itself when a vocal political group within the United Kingdom, one of the founding members of the European Union, expressed great skepticism about the long-term benefits of EU membership. Eventually this movement, known as Brexit, led to a national referendum in 2016 in which the British people by a razor-thin margin voted in favor of the United Kingdom leaving the European Union. The Brexit vote came as a shock to many, because Britain had been an EU member for forty-seven years and during that time had exerted great influence over the EU's direction. It took four years to negotiate the actual withdrawal, and Brexit became effective in 2020.

The trend toward nationalism in Europe gained new traction in November 2016 when, to the surprise of many political pundits, Donald Trump was elected the forty-fifth president of the United States. Both as president and earlier during his campaign, Trump pushed his MAGA ("Make America Great Again") platform. Trump was far less supportive of the European Union than were any prior U.S. presidents. During his tenure in the White House, America's historical support for the NATO military alliance and the European Union diminished as Trump openly questioned their value to U.S. national security interests. Many Trump supporters were (and are to this day) individuals who, like those in Europe, believed that the tangible benefits of globalization had passed them by. Often those individuals were former blue-collar laborers who had watched their well-paid American manufacturing jobs be offshored to Asia (particularly to China) beginning in the late 1980s. The massive trade deficits that America ran up with countries around the world, the largest of course being China, were a direct result of these offshored and outsourced American jobs. During his four years in office, Trump also questioned, and in some cases directly backed away from, America's historical long-term financial commitments and support for international organizations such as the World Health Organization (WHO).

COVID-19: GASOLINE ON THE EMBERS

Things became worse in early 2020 when a fast-spreading pandemic engulfed the entire world. Few foresaw or anticipated the massive political, social, and economic upheavals as COVID-19 emerged first in China, moved rapidly through Asia, then to Europe, and later swept across North and South America. As hospitals around the world filled to capacity and death rates spiked, nations experienced dangerously inadequate supplies of ventilators, surgical masks, personal protective equipment (PPE), and other medical necessities. National political leaders were confronted by angry voters as they realized—too late—that the critical medical products their constituents desperately needed to fight the virus were not manufactured, either in whole or in part, within their own countries. The United States is a prime example.

In the midst of a global pandemic, people questioned how offshored medical products could suddenly become unavailable. The answer is simple. Manufacturers two decades earlier had adopted the wildly popular "just-in-time" inventory philosophy originally conceived in Japan. Simply put, necessary production components sourced from third parties were scheduled to arrive "just in time" to complete the manufacturing process. Less inventory equals less overhead costs. Also, the financial gurus in large companies believed they could boost their earnings before interest, taxes, depreciation, and amortization (EBITDA) by offshoring manufacturing capabilities. Nice theory if everything works in perfect unison, including transportation and warehousing. Why waste cash on inventory just sitting in warehouses? However, like a very expensive mechanical watch, just-in-time manufacturing only works until there is a broken or unavailable part, and then the entire process grinds to a halt.

The years 2020 and 2021 will be forever marked by consumer panic over shelves empty of toilet paper, cleaning supplies, and popular food and baking items. But three years later, the global supply chain remains largely dysfunctional with little relief in sight. Because reliance on just-in-time manufacturing still exists, the global supply chain will never again return to what was once considered normal. Frankly, I believe the world is just one global event away from returning to where we were at the height of the pandemic.

Nationalism accelerated during the COVID-19 pandemic as global shortages of critical medical supplies forced governments around the world to respond to the panic-driven demands of their constituents. Politicians began to seriously reevaluate whether products that had previously been outsourced should be partially—or entirely—manufactured within their own borders. Protecting national security interests by regulating where key goods are produced was viewed as a tangible step politicians could take to prop up their popularity among a disenchanted populace. None of this came as welcome news to China, which over three decades had become rich as it built up its economy on the backs of inbound investments from Europe, North America, and parts of Asia.

CHINA'S CLOSING DOOR AND AMERICA'S REACTION

This was all occurring at the same time Xi Jinping decided to escalate centralized control over the Chinese economy in ways that heretofore had never been done. For three decades prior, China had aggressively promoted an "open-arms" investment policy that encouraged investments from literally anywhere as a means to grow its economy and manufacturing base. However, Xi Jinping is reversing that policy, and China's trading partners are reacting.

The United States, of course, has a number of problems with China's growing nationalism. National security interests and the risks posed by foreign investors buying or investing in U.S. companies have been an ongoing concern for the U.S. Congress and policymakers going back generations (such as America's reactions to Japan during its bubble period from 1986 to 1992). In fact, the warnings about foreign investment can be traced back to the founding of America. George Washington, America's first president, recognized early on that if the newly formed America were to survive, it had to develop its own self-sufficient manufacturing base. Washington felt this was essential so America could avoid the risk of once again being subject to foreign control and influences from Europe. He foresaw the future by warning that America must become more than merely a consumer economy and demanding dependence on its own resources and technology. Unfortunately, few presidents who followed Washington heeded this advice.

Concerns over national security rose to a high level of priority during the Trump Administration, leading to the strengthening of the U.S. government review mechanism known as the Committee on Foreign Investment in the United States (CFIUS). CFIUS is the high-level U.S. government interagency task force that has the authority to oversee proposed foreign investments in the United States. It is composed of official representatives from the Departments of Homeland Security, Justice, Defense, Treasury, Commerce, State, and Energy, along with members of the Office of U.S. Trade Representatives and the Office of Science and Technology Policy. The job of CFIUS is to monitor transactions both large and small that have the potential to impact U.S. security interests. Through the president, CFIUS has the power to approve or disapprove a proposed foreign investment involving the United States or even reverse an already completed deal if it is found to be contrary to U.S. policy or to national security.

The growing role of CFIUS has the potential to impact all foreign companies and individuals considering investments in the United States. CFIUS has continued to expand its reach but has carved out exceptions for certain countries that it considers to be close American allies. On that list are Canada, Australia, the United Kingdom, and, as of February 2022, New Zealand, which was granted an "accepted foreign state designation." While this is temporary in nature, it is expected to be expanded. The point is to designate key allies in areas where national security interests of the United States are not expected to be seriously challenged. In August 2023, President Biden signed an Executive Order that expanded the role of CFIUS to include outbound investments and technology transfers to China for key national security products and technologies.[2] Even state legislatures are getting into the act by passing laws to limit or in some cases prohibit the sale of farmland to non–U.S. citizens or companies.

NATION-STATES EMBRACING FOREIGN DIRECT INVESTMENT REGIMES

The United States is not alone in imposing foreign direct investment (FDI) restrictions. Both the European Union and China are imposing their own sets of laws and regulations similar to CFIUS to monitor foreign investment. In Canada, Western Europe, and Japan, the opportunities for foreign direct investment are becoming more restricted as governments reevaluate national security needs. Each country adopts its own unique approach to monitoring investments coming from other countries. Their review processes generally dictate whether to initially flag a transaction or to require further screening based on a myriad of factors.[3] [4]

The unexpected emergence of COVID-19 was like throwing gasoline on burning embers; it ignited the already smoldering global movement toward FDI restrictions. Several countries had already been lowering thresholds across some industries, but as COVID-19 began to wreak economic havoc, countries began to fear foreign investors would be tempted to buy struggling domestic companies, thus weakening the host country's economy. As a result, a worldwide MaxTrend® emerged that applied broad definitions to potential FDI transactions in order to implement stronger restrictions. The key point I wish to emphasize here is that increased nationalism (i.e., the nation-state mentality) is directly prompting stronger and more widely embraced restrictions on foreign direct investment. This acts as a brake on FDI transactions that in the past would take place easily and with less governmental interference. Most countries now require a "pretransaction notification" that brings certain types of foreign direct investments under review. Under broader parameters of what is considered a national interest, transactions with companies producing personal protective equipment in most cases fall under mandatory governmental review. The rationale is that public health concerns demand government involvement. As each country reviews FDI transactions, it evaluates whether a transaction is detrimental to public interest. While these increased restrictions are not all the result of COVID-19, countries have been more aggressive in seeking to avoid further economic harm.

It is naive to believe that nations will loosen their FDI restrictions anytime soon. As countries try to reclaim their own domestic industries, multinational deals will become less predictable. Restrictions are unlikely to weaken, particularly in protected sectors.

A DETERRENT TO OUTSIDE INVESTING

No nation over the last century has benefited more from an open, multilateral free trade system than China. While the United States lost over seven million manufacturing jobs, China's economy grew spectacularly, at times between 6 and 12 percent. The icing on the cake for China was its official and hard-fought-for admission to the World

Trade Organization (WTO) in 2001. China has emerged as the world's premium manufacturing center and wants to retain the title.

After a decade of building up its economy as a WTO member, China began to reevaluate its priorities. Both incoming and outgoing foreign investment began to be more closely scrutinized. This trend accelerated after Xi Jinping became the leader of China. For Xi, national security takes a higher priority than growing China's manufacturing capacities. Xi has erected barriers for inbound and outbound investments while at the same time aggressively promoting and funding China's Belt and Road Initiative, which seems quite a paradox.

The key point China has failed to appreciate is that, with the return of nationalism, its ability to attract inbound investment is becoming seriously limited. Nation-states by their nature are inward-looking. The United States and Canada, as well as countries in Europe and elsewhere, have adopted what China had done—that is, carefully considering inbound investments and how they might impact domestic economies. Countries also recognize that their national security interests may be fatally weakened if they have an economy that is totally controlled by external events. This is why the phrase "national security" continues to raise concerns around the world. While things were already moving in that direction, the COVID-19 crisis hit. When nations lacked respirators, masks, and the vaccines required to fight the virus, they realized their vulnerabilities, and national security was no longer a theoretical goal. All of this promises to weaken China's ability to support its internal growth simultaneously with its external policies.

Also China, like other more developed countries, needs to accept the fact that while a young nation's economy can grow quickly, inevitably external factors slow the process. A good example of this is Chinese labor. China was able to encourage inbound investment because Chinese labor in the 1980s and 1990s was both inexpensive and efficient. Times have changed, and Chinese labor is no longer inexpensive. All of this means that Xi Jinping, in abandoning the policies of his predecessors and looking more inward, is weakening China's ability to grow its economy as quickly as it might wish. China now faces the challenge of asserting itself in a world of nation-states far more focused on their own needs. The ride for China is about to get a lot tougher.

CHAPTER FOURTEEN

THE FRUSTRATING STRUGGLE FOR TECH/INNOVATION DOMINANCE

Xi Jinping is passionate about China developing its own homegrown technologies to surpass the West. Some Chinese companies such as Alibaba Group, Tencent Holdings Ltd., and ByteDance have been successful. But even these successful tech companies are limited in how they can use their technology and where they can do business. Spreading their tech to other countries is challenging because the Chinese government demands they keep their technologies private. Equally concerning is how the Chinese government has imposed so many mandatory regulations for tech companies and their owners (both domestic and foreign) that it actually discourages innovation. As the United States has learned, innovation most often emerges from smaller, more entrepreneurial companies, not the large corporations. China apparently hasn't realized this, and it has inadvertently erected roadblocks for those in China who might otherwise develop creative new technologies. Nevertheless, the more China remains dependent on Western technologies, the less likely it is to realize its world-leading vision.

"Technology" is an inexact term that describes those ideas and inventions that have the potential to change and hopefully improve our lives. Perhaps the earliest "invention" was when our distant ancestors picked up sticks and madly waved them around to keep wild animals at bay, but the one invention that truly changed the world was the wheel. No one really knows how or when the wheel first appeared. One group of archaeologists believe the concept of the wheel emerged sometime around 8000 BCE in Asia. Other scholars credit Mesopotamia between 3000 and 5000 BCE. Regardless of its origin, using a wheel, at first for grinding grain and later for transportation by adding axles so objects could easily move from one location to another, truly changed the course of human history.

The critical role technology plays in fostering economic power has not been lost on Xi Jinping and the current Chinese leadership. Xi clearly recognizes that China's fostering of technological innovation is indispensable to its future. However, what frustrates Xi is that most of the products China manufactures for export are dependent upon Western-based technologies.

Over the last thirty-five years, the world has seen the single-chip microprocessor evolve to become increasingly sophisticated and widespread, the establishment of the World Wide Web, the development of quantum computing (which morphed into the personal computer and cell phones), the creation of the Linux operating system, high-definition televisions, nanotechnology, the DeepMind artificial intelligence computer program, tremendous advances in medical technology—the list is endless. The global impact of these technologies has made companies such as Apple, Microsoft, Dell, Sony, and Intel household names. China's frustration is that most of these technologies have Western origins. As a result, many technology giants are headquartered in America. Right after he came to power in 2013, Xi decreed that China must focus its resources on first replicating Western technologies and then creating technologies of its own. While China wants to replace Western technologies, it recognizes that the West and particularly the United States has had a huge head start. Xi's dream is a "two-technology world"—one Chinese and the other Western—where China no longer depends on the West.

ENTER VENTURE CAPITAL

How did America manage to attain such a technological lead over so many other countries over the last forty years? The simplest answer is *venture capital.* For example, many American companies involved in genetic and medical technologies over the last four decades were heavily funded by venture capitalists. In the 1970s, venture capital emerged as a new phenomenon. Today, the amount of money in the United States under management in privately controlled venture funds is about $550 billion. Sounds like a lot, but it really isn't when you consider the amount of investments in more traditional areas (such as stock markets) is over $50 *trillion.* This means that less than 1 percent of the funds available for aggressive long-term investments are directed by a relative handful of venture capitalists. While the U.S. government has historically underwritten critical research through entities such as the National Science Foundation, the National Institute of Health, and DARPA (the Defense Advanced Research Projects Agency), private venture capital throughout has played an outsized role in fostering true innovation.

Over the last decade, Western and some Asian-based venture capitalists have increasingly targeted opportunities in China. The downside for Chinese leadership is that as Chinese companies such as Tencent Holdings Ltd., Alibaba Group, and ByteDance have become highly successful, they have simultaneously become politically and economically powerful and are thus viewed with concern by the Chinese Communist Party. Those Chinese companies have aggressively pursued opportunities to both identify technologies developed in China and at the same time seek out targets for investment outside of China. This poses a challenge for the current Chinese leadership, as its goal is to sequester technology within China's borders for its own benefit.

CHINA'S EFFORTS TO CONTROL TECH COMPANIES

In response to this dilemma, Xi Jinping and the Chinese government have become increasingly active by imposing restrictions on where and how Chinese tech companies are permitted to invest and seek out key technologies. Remember that China's leadership covets Chinese-based, not Western-based, technologies. An interesting article by Keith Zhi titled "Chinese Tech Companies Warned of Tighter Rules on Investments" (*Wall Street Journal*, January 20, 2022) highlighted how Chinese officials cannot resist constantly promulgating new rules requiring Chinese technology companies to apply for "pre-approval" before making investment deals. One example is the strict regulatory role imposed by the Cyberspace Administration of China. Basically, for the largest China-based tech companies, formal government preclearance for investment deals has become the norm. While undoubtedly things will continue to change after this book is published, Chinese tech companies will in my opinion remain a constant irritant for powerful Chinese government officials. Even leading Chinese tech companies such as Tencent Holdings Ltd., Alibaba Group, and ByteDance have been subjected to the broad reach of these regulators. I have little doubt that the highly driven and successful Chinese innovators behind these companies are very frustrated competing not just in China but in highly competitive global markets. The problem is there is no way they can object to or successfully counteract Chinese regulations they feel are overly restrictive. If they were Western-based companies, they would have more options.

NO LIMITS ON CHINESE TRUSTBUSTERS

Because of their potential economic and political impact, technology companies in China are under their government's microscope, much as American companies were beginning in the 20th century. Over one hundred years ago, massive growth and expansion took place in the American steel, mining, railroad, and energy industries. The U.S. Congress and the "trustbusters" back then feared that gigantic industrial corporations in strategic sectors, and particularly the individuals running them, posed a threat of becoming more powerful than the U.S. government itself. This led to the passage of far-reaching federal antitrust laws (such as the Sherman Antitrust Act of 1890) designed to curb the growing power and reach of America's largest corporations. While these new antitrust laws did for a time blunt the influence of these corporations, these restrictions were reined in by federal court limitations on the ability of the U.S. government to impose and enforce those laws. Also, large corporations (Standard Oil, owned by the Rockefeller family, is an apt example) were able to exert incredible political influence over government policymakers, and Congress ended up weakening any regulations the U.S. government attempted to impose on the private sector companies.

Unlike early 20th-century America, no limitations exist in China today on what policies Xi Jinping and CCP officials may or may not decide to impose on foreign and domestic companies doing business in China. Thus, all tech companies in China have no alternative but to accept whatever policies China's central government wishes to impose. This is why the edicts of the Cyberspace Administration of China and other regulatory bodies within the Chinese government have the power to directly influence the future of how and where Chinese tech companies can operate.

THE DILEMMA OF REGULATION

This brings us to the fundamental dilemma facing Xi Jinping and Chinese regulators. Is it wise to place top-down restraints on tech companies in a country that is looking to expand its technology base and global reach? And further, will this stifle those companies from developing their own technologies independent of the West? The answer lies in how best to foster a climate that encourages innovation by Chinese individuals and companies. A key lesson China could learn from America's experience is that large corporations[1] have generally *not* been sources of significant innovation. The reality is, many revolutionary technologies have emerged out of smaller and entrepreneurial companies (this is true in both the U.S. and Europe). While many small tech companies ultimately fail, those that do succeed end up as the source of opportunities for larger corporations. From the 1950s through the 1980s, larger U.S. companies were more prone to focusing on R&D within their own structures. Eventually, though, CEOs recognized that the return on the capital invested in their internal R&D departments was unpredictable, which made a strategy of acquiring small tech companies a much sounder bet. This institutionalized the legions of mergers and acquisitions (M&A) lawyers and consultants who made a game out of having large corporations swallow up the small companies, and who made the smart venture capitalists rich.

This led to geometric growth of the venture capital industry throughout the United States, and venture capital is now actively seeking out targets around the world. The most successful venture capitalists manage to identify and then develop critical new and emerging technologies. Places like Silicon Valley in California, the Boston technology ring, and lesser-known pockets of innovation such as the venture capital activity created by Carnegie Mellon University graduates in Pittsburgh, have led the way to countless successful technological developments.

To the surprise of many observers, including myself, the COVID-19 crisis did not suppress venture capital funding. In fact, in 2021, the Asian region (which includes China) attracted more than $165 billion in venture capital investments—50 percent higher than when the pandemic began in 2020. Unlike the U.S. model, though, much of that Asian investment seemed directed toward late-stage or established technology growth companies rather than smaller emerging tech companies.

Chinese government regulators remain concerned about the potential economic and political influence that the technology giants in China can exert globally. This is why it should have come as no surprise how Chinese regulators reacted when the Chinese ride-sharing company Didi went forward with its planned initial public offering in

June 2021. After the Chinese regulators expressed unhappiness with the move, Beijing intervened by ordering the company to suspend new user applications. The result was that Didi shares fell by more than one-third after its initial public offering. In other sectors, the Chinese government's dissatisfaction with private schools and after-school tutoring in China had an immediate impact on those entities. And as discussed elsewhere in this book, the failed real estate sector in light of the Evergrande crisis in 2021 (which was followed by the missteps of Country Garden in 2023) prompted strong intervention by the Chinese government.

The unanswered question is simply this: Can Chinese government officials continue to exert a dominant regulatory role over Chinese technology companies and at the same time expect that this will not counteract China's goal of becoming a global leader in innovations? From the overriding experience of the United States, the answer is no. Developing and possessing successful technology is not just a matter of the availability of sufficient venture capital. Companies and the creative types who work in them have to be unrestricted to be able to act independently and focus on the technologies they believe are most valuable. Money alone is not enough.

A related development is that in order to protect their domestic technologies, many companies are aggressively restricting the ability of foreign companies (particularly Chinese) to acquire those technologies. Thus, access to technologies internationally is being greatly diminished. As China pursues its Made in China 2025[2] policy as well as its Belt and Road Initiative, an increasingly restrictive technology pool will impact not just private industries but also China's state-owned enterprises. Without a doubt, China faces major challenges ahead.

CHAPTER FIFTEEN

REJECTING FOREIGN INVESTMENT

Years ago, someone said to me, "If you have a million dollars and a clean bowling shirt, you can do business in China." From the mid-1980s to around 2010, this was true. China was a wide-open country that actively embraced all kinds of foreign investment, fueling China's unprecedented three decades of economic growth. "Everyone is welcome" and "Anything goes" was the policy, and the world's largest corporations, particularly those based in the United States, Europe, and Japan, poured trillions of dollars, yen, and euros into a vast swath of Chinese industries. Starting in 2011, though, China's door began to close. Particularly after Xi Jinping took control in 2013, China became increasingly wary of foreign investment for a number of reasons. At first this development was triggered by China's deteriorating military and economic relationship with the United States; later it accelerated due to the Trump-era tariffs, which are still in place today. A wide range of new, restrictive policies have since been enacted by Chinese authorities, forbidding foreign investment near military sites and severely limiting or altogether preventing investment from outside companies seeking control of Chinese industries. The Unreliable Entity List, essentially a blacklist of foreign companies deemed unsuitable as investors in China, soon followed. These and other government-imposed policies have contributed to the slowing of China's growth and promise to slow it even further in the future.

China is now in the midst of rejecting the policies that were so successfully implemented by Deng Xiaoping and his successors (prior to Xi Jinping), which have been largely responsible for China's enormous wealth accumulation and historic growth over the last forty years. This reversal is due to Xi Jinping's preference for implementing his own political doctrines that emphasize centralized political control over open-ended economic policies.

In order to better understand what is going on, look back to the time Mao ruled China. During his reign from 1949 until his death in 1976, Mao Zedong—a true autocrat—forcefully imposed on the Chinese people his xenophobic philosophies that unfortunately led to his disastrous Great Leap Forward vision for China and other failures. Even after Mao died in 1976, China remained a closed and desperately poor economy. Back then, visitors to Beijing would encounter massive traffic clogged with millions of pedestrians and bicycles, overcrowded buses, and very occasionally black cars ferrying around high-level Chinese Communist Party officials. China was a wreck.

A brief sign of hope appeared during the early 1970s when a then-popular President Richard Nixon in a surprise move visited Beijing and abruptly reversed America's long-standing policy on China. Pundits at the time predicted a rapid rise for the Chinese economy as they expected the trade relationship between the United States and China to open wide. They were wrong; Mao was still firmly in charge. Change would only be possible after Mao was out of power.

DENG XIAOPING'S PROPHETIC VISION FOR CHINA

It was only after Mao died in 1976 that things slowly began to improve. Deng Xiaoping rose to become the leader of the PRC in late 1978, and over the next eleven years aggressively implemented real change. Deng recognized that China's infrastructure was nearly nonexistent, and that in order for it to grow, China desperately needed access to vast amounts of capital to modernize its economy and industries, many of which were state-owned enterprises. Because the capital needed to fund this transformation could not be generated within China, Deng decided to base his plans on making a "deal" with the SOEs and the few private entities and entrepreneurs then existing in China. The deal was simply this: China's political elite would permit them to run their businesses as quasi-capitalistic enterprises as long as they agreed to never become involved in politics. In short, "Stay out of politics and we'll leave you alone." Chinese businesses and nascent entrepreneurs got the message and embraced the deal. After that, everything changed.

To kickstart Deng's unprecedented policy, the Chinese government created and funded special economic zones. Beginning in the Pearl River Delta located in Southern China and then spreading throughout the country, the SEZs were centers devoted to private enterprise and encouraging investments by foreign entities. The results were astounding. To highlight how successful this policy was, China's gross domestic product in 1985 was $309.5 billion. In the year 1995 it was $734.5 billion; in 2000 it was $1.211 trillion; in 2010 it was $6.087 trillion; and in 2022 it was $17.8 trillion. This was only possible because of the huge influx of yen, dollars, euros, and other currencies pouring into China as foreign companies and investors moved their sourcing for manufactured goods to Chinese factories. China's unprecedented growth was simply a matter of mathematics—if you grow an economy at about 8.5 percent per year, in eight to nine years the economy will double. China has proven that again and again and again. Today, China has the second largest economy in the world, next only to the United States.

XI'S NEW PRIORITIES FOR REGULATING FOREIGN DIRECT INVESTMENT

Largely due to Deng Xiaoping's "deal," from 1980 to 2010 China was wide open and embraced whatever foreign investment happened to come along. This enabled China to accumulate trillions in foreign hard currencies that were redirected by the Chinese government to pay for infrastructure projects throughout China. These projects included the refabrication and/or construction of airports, seaports, high-speed railroads, and an extensive highway network rivaling the interstate highway system the United States constructed during the 1950s. The Chinese government has always wanted to attract foreign investors that own or control technologies that China needs, so as to advance the sophistication of Chinese technologies in emerging industries. Foreign investors found themselves aggressively courted by provincial officials, and a result China amassed both wealth and valuable technologies, and its economy exponentially grew.

THE SPECTER OF RUSSIAN OLIGARCHS AND CHINA

Despite what you read, China and Russia have never really been close allies. As China carefully monitored the disintegration of the USSR in the late 1980s, it took away two important lessons. First, it was obvious to the Chinese leadership how dysfunctional Russia became in the 1990s after it lost control of its currency. Russia's economy faltered and even today is far too dependent on just a few commodities, oil being the biggest player. Second, and what I believe was an even bigger lesson for the Chinese, was the impact created by the rapid rise of the extremely wealthy and potentially powerful Russian oligarchs. Billionaire oligarchs gained the ability to operate independently within Russia and represented then, and now, a potential political challenge to Russia's leadership.

Recognizing how this developed in Russia, the amazing success experienced by billionaire Chinese entrepreneurs over the last decade was not lost on the CCP leadership. Could the same happen in China? Some experts calculate that there are more billionaires today in China than in the United States. After Xi Jinping assumed power in 2013, there is little doubt that he kept a close eye on the Chinese equivalent of the Russian oligarchs. One widely publicized example is China's Jack Ma, a billionaire who cofounded the highly successful Alibaba Group and later cofounded the Chinese private equity group Yunfeng Capital. At one point Ma was ranked as the richest individual in China. As Xi Jinping methodically consolidated the power of the CCP, the economic and potential political power that business leaders like Jack Ma could exercise in China (such as Ma's efforts to transform the tech corporation Ant Group by public offerings in Shanghai and Hong Kong) became clear. Because of this accumulation of power, 2021 saw a regulatory crackdown on Ma's businesses. In July 2023, Ant and its subsidiaries were fined slightly less than $1 billion by Chinese security regulators. This is just one of numerous examples of how Chinese companies continue to be systematically reined in by China's central regulatory authorities.

CHINA'S WANING EMBRACE OF FOREIGN INVESTMENT

Following the very successful 2008 Olympic Games in Beijing, China began to adopt a new posture in its drive to become a global player. Around 2011, China's historical open investment policy slowly began to reverse. An important indication of what was to come occurred when China's Ministry of Commerce together with China's powerful National Development and Reform Commission (NDRC) established a set of rules that introduced the idea of a formalized security review. This move was designed to examine significant incoming foreign investments to China and to determine whether specific transactions were in China's best economic and political interests. Under those 2011 rules, and more that followed, an official panel in China was given broad discretionary powers to perform National Security Reviews when foreign companies sought permission to invest in domestic Chinese companies. Implemented slowly at first and then moving more quickly, the 2011 rules were expanded under China's National Security Law in 2015. Then, after the Trump Administration took office in 2017 and China–U.S. relations worsened as tariffs were imposed by both sides, the prospect of future foreign direct investments in China, particularly in key industries, worried Chinese officials.

China accelerated its efforts to scrutinize foreign investors in 2020 when the Measures for Security Review of Foreign Investments were formally issued by China's Ministry of Commerce (MOFCOM) and the NDRC. This was a significant step for the Chinese for a number of reasons. First, the 2020 regulations were broader in scope than either the 2011 or 2015 rules. The previous rules were intended to limit investments that might be in close proximity to Chinese military properties or where foreign investors were seeking total control of Chinese enterprises. Second, the 2020 regulations expanded the concept of "pre-review" beyond traditional areas, which meant that increasing numbers of Chinese entities were subject to prior government approval when seeking out foreign investors. This meant the National Security Review system became a national as opposed to a more provincial law, with a broader scope of control. Beyond that, in late 2020, MOFCOM further extended its reach by promulgating what is called the Unreliable Entity List (UEL). Basically, the UEL determines which companies are or might be prohibited from investing in China. A year later, China established the PRC Data Security Law (DSL), arguing that data security is critically important to the Chinese government's ability to control China's economy. Then, the Cyberspace Administration of China entered the ring by adding types of transactions involving cybersecurity that would trigger a review in China. Although this is only a brief summary of what occurred over ten years, it provides a picture of how radically policies have changed under Xi Jinping.

CRACKING DOWN ON FOREIGN INVESTORS

Today the purview of Chinese authorities to approve or deny foreign investments is much broader than what exists in the United States under the authority of the Committee on Foreign Investment in the United States (CFIUS). My guess is the Chinese carefully studied how CFIUS operates in the U.S. and then refined and adapted the concept to a Chinese model. There is no doubt that the Chinese scope of reviews will become even more comprehensive going forward. This means future market access to China will inevitably shrink for non-Chinese investors. As this book is being published, the Chinese government is continuing to update and further refine its laws on restricting foreign direct investment. The $64,000 question is whether China can impose these restrictive types of laws and at the same time still attract the kind of advanced technology-focused investments it so desires.

There are both overt and less obvious signs that foreign companies currently operating in China are targets of Chinese regulators. In 2023, Chinese authorities carried out a series of raids on a number of foreign "advisory companies" that were conducting a brisk business of providing market information on China and its economy to their foreign clients. Chinese authorities are systematically tightening access to the kind of information that investors outside China really need to properly evaluate their present or potential Chinese investments and any political risks. One prominent example is China's new counter-espionage law that came into effect on July 1, 2023. A tool for China to crack down on foreign investors, this law threatens to punish any non-Chinese company or individual currently doing business in China if authorities determine the individual or company is transferring information that potentially impinges on Chinese national security interests. According to a publicly available report released by America's National Counterintelligence and Security Center (NCSC), China's new counterespionage law provides Chinese officials "expanded legal grounds for accessing and controlling data held by U.S. firms in China." This lays to rest any question that China is increasingly promoting its national security over economic interests.

Since the counterespionage law is ambiguous as to what constitutes "national security secrets," Chinese authorities have the unilateral power to determine on a case-by-case basis if *any* document or data could potentially come under the purview of the new law. This creates a chilling effect on Western companies now operating in China, regardless of the type of business. For example, in 2023, Chinese authorities raided a number of Western advisory groups located in China, including Bain & Company and the Mintz Group. Another concern facing Western companies operating in China is that Chinese authorities could potentially use the counterespionage law as an excuse to approach Chinese employees working for such Western companies. Specifically, Chinese authorities could "encourage" those employees to pass along confidential information, either formally or informally. Either way, this is all bad news for Western companies in China. During 2023, as this new counterespionage law was being put into effect, Xi Jinping and Chinese officials were holding highly publicized meetings with well-known Western business executives like Bill Gates, Jamie Dimon, and others.

China's current leadership is adopting aggressive steps to make foreign investment in China as difficult as possible, and may well succeed. Ironically, though, this will undercut China's ability to achieve its long-term goals. According to the *Wall Street Journal*, Sequoia Capital, a powerful technology investment group, announced that by March 2024 it is going to split into three independent firms located in the United States, India, and China to avoid ongoing geopolitical concerns. This is occurring as increased pressure is coming from Washington, DC, on American companies pursuing investments in China that may affect U.S. national security. Can China crack down on foreign investors and still maintain a vibrant economy? Only time will tell.

INVESTMENT MIGRATION TO OTHER COUNTRIES

The challenge for Xi Jinping is to maintain China's status as the global manufacturing powerhouse that it has built, out of nothing, over the last forty years. The fact that the Chinese are now cracking down on both domestic as well as foreign companies in China makes it difficult to imagine how the current administration under Xi can preserve the balance it so desires. This new reality is forcing foreign companies and investors to seriously evaluate the advisability of pursuing business opportunities in China. Some high-profile U.S. companies that have already made massive investments in China may be able to work out special deals because of their size and importance to the Chinese economy. However, for many Western companies, doing business in China poses increasingly significant risks, and this is particularly crucial if China is a sole-source supplier to those companies. Even Apple has publicly announced plans to expand some operations outside China, one major beneficiary being India. At a minimum, any European or North American company currently sourcing out of China needs to seriously consider the advisability of identifying at least one backup source outside China as insurance against future political disputes that are likely to arise between China and the West. Though the challenge is clear, exactly how Xi Jinping intends to counterbalance this MaxTrend® is yet to be seen.

CHAPTER SIXTEEN

INTELLECTUAL PROPERTY
What Goes Around Comes Around

They marvel much to hear, that gold, which in itself is so useless, should be everywhere so much sought, that even for men, for whom it was made, and by them hath its value, should be less esteemed.

— Sir Thomas More, *Utopia, Book 2*
"Utopian View of Riches, Gold, and Jewels" (1516)

Since man's early origins, the desire to possess gold has been a universal obsession. Gold was once viewed as the ultimate symbol of power and wealth. Governments amassed vast quantities of gold to finance their economies and political ambitions. Until the mid-20th century, leading national currencies were directly tied to how much physical gold was housed in national treasuries. But five hundred years ago, Sir Thomas More got it right when he described gold as something "which in itself is so useless." Today, rather than gold, what truly represents a nation's strength is its ability to innovate and control technologies. Technology is the "gold" of the 21st century, and unless those who own a technology can prevent others from stealing or misappropriating it, its value is lost. The legal mechanism designed to shield valuable technologies from theft is known as "intellectual property" (IP) protection, which takes the form of patents, trademarks, copyrights, and trade secrets.

While intellectual property protection is a high priority today for both America's Democratic and Republican Parties, this was not always the case. I once worked in the U.S. Senate for Senator Hugh D. Scott who, in addition to being the Senate Republican Minority Leader, served as the Vice Chair of the Senate Subcommittee on Patents, Trademarks, and Copyrights. One day significant revisions to U.S. patent laws were being debated on the floor of the Senate, but, not surprisingly, very few senators were actually present.[1] Senator Scott, known for his calm demeanor and very dry sense of humor, stood up and thanked his few colleagues for their attendance for what he considered to be a very important bill. Then he said (paraphrasing to the best of my memory), "I am very grateful for those of you here today, because if the top priorities for most of your constituents rank from one to one hundred, with one being the most important, then the patent law updates we are debating today are probably number ninety-nine." Senator Scott's point was that while most of his colleagues at the time did not realize (or care) about strengthening patent laws, they should have. In the 1970s, it was the expansion and enforcement of U.S. antitrust laws that were viewed as a top legislative priority for Congress, not patents and copyrights. More than four decades later, priorities have completely reversed in both the Senate and House of Representatives. Given the critical role technology plays in growing America's economy, the importance of protecting intellectual property no longer wallows at "number ninety-nine"—it is now in the top five.

An individual's right to intellectual property is basically a Western concept. The U.S. Constitution directly guarantees the right to own intellectual property and mandates that the U.S. government protect the rights of inventors and property holders. Over the last two hundred years, the concept of protecting intellectual property was aggressively exported to the rest of world by the United States and several other Western nations and made part of their national laws.

HOW CHINA VIEWS INTELLECTUAL PROPERTY

This brings us to how China and its leadership view intellectual property. China, like many other countries, particularly in Asia, has historically been reluctant (to say the least) about embracing the concept of intellectual property. This is a key reason why it is common for disputes to arise between Chinese officials and non-Chinese intellectual property owners who have located their manufacturing facilities in China. China's sheer reluctance to enforce intellectual property laws has often enabled Chinese companies to "encourage" (compel) non-Chinese companies to reveal their valuable technologies, even if those technologies are protected by patents, trademarks, or copyrights.[2]

For years, I personally found it difficult to comprehend exactly why the Chinese devalue intellectual property protection to such a great extent. By chance, I met a scientist who was born in China, and he helped me to understand why. After earning his PhD in chemistry, this scientist left China for the United States to work for a major international oil company. In a conversation over dinner one evening, I asked him why the Chinese were so reluctant to recognize the concept of intellectual property protection. He responded with a personal story:

> As a young child, I lived in a very rural area of China. There were no hospitals or medical facilities within easy reach. So, every six or seven weeks, a doctor would come to our village to see patients and dispense medicine. Once there was a very sick child in the village. After examining the child, the traveling doctor prepared a secret formula to treat the child. Unfortunately, the medicine spoiled quickly and had to be remixed every few days. Because the doctor only came to the village every six weeks or so, this meant the parents would not have enough medicine to treat their child. The parents begged the doctor to reveal the formula so they could

make it themselves, but the doctor refused, saying they would steal the formula and then it would no longer be his. The desperate family insisted that they would not do this and promised to keep the formula a secret. Eventually, the doctor reluctantly revealed the formula, emphatically making the parents swear they would never disclose it to anyone. When the doctor left, the parents mixed the medicine, and the child got better. After that, the parents began to tell the secret formula to others in the village.

Confused, I asked him to explain to me the point of his story. Hadn't the parents broken their promise and essentially stolen the secret formula? He replied, "Yes, but isn't it more important that the formula be freely shared to benefit many families rather than be owned by just one person?" In his way of thinking, the parents had done nothing wrong.

For decades, China has made protecting intellectual property particularly difficult for foreign investors and companies. This is especially true when it comes to trade secrets. While a valid patent can guarantee protection for a limited period of time (seventeen to twenty years), it is different for trade secrets. A trade secret, if handled properly, can essentially be kept a secret forever.[3]

The Chinese government over the last decade under the direction of Xi Jinping has drastically increased governmental intervention in the activities of both domestic and foreign companies operating in China. This policy poses a particular threat for those companies that greatly rely on their own specialized and proprietary technologies. Non-Chinese companies often find themselves forced to disclose valuable corporate information if they wish to continue doing business in China. One common practice is to pressure foreign companies to work with Chinese entities as joint venture partners and to disclose their technologies in order to stay in the game. Also, whenever foreign companies try to do business with Chinese state-owned enterprises, non-Chinese technology owners should expect to find themselves pressured to disclose confidential information if they want future business.

XI JINPING'S DILEMMA

Xi Jinping and China's leadership are only now beginning to realize there is a real downside to their practice of ferreting out intellectual property from non-Chinese companies through any means. Increasing numbers of foreign companies, unwilling to risk their valuable information, are deciding against doing business in China. Some that were operating in China have already left.

Another, even more serious challenge for China's leadership is that as more and more Chinese companies look to market their products and technologies outside of China, they are demanding that their own patents and trademarks be respected around the world. What some Chinese have encountered instead is retaliation by the governments and industries of those nations that have been harmed in the past by China's lack of respect for intellectual property rights. What, then, is the price to China's economy and its international reputation? Ultimately, China's access to the Western-based technologies it needs will be diminished because it refuses to recognize and honor the proprietary rights of others.

SECTION III

WHAT THE WEST MUST DO

The next six chapters describe what steps the West, and particularly the United States, must take if they want to blunt Xi Jinping's and China's ambitious agenda. China is both determined and capable. To take China for granted is a big mistake.

CHAPTER SEVENTEEN

DOUBLE DOWN ON A BLUE-WATER STRATEGY

A "blue water" capability means a nation can project itself both defensively and offensively, not just in the coastal regions surrounding its home borders, but throughout the world. As of 2024, only one country possesses a true blue-water capability, and that is the United States. The U.S. Navy since 1945 has been particularly dominant throughout the Pacific Theater and in South Asian waters. China is not happy about this and desperately wants to amass its own blue-water capabilities so as to eventually replace the U.S. naval presence throughout the region. China's efforts to bring the South China Sea and surrounding areas under its control pose an ongoing threat to world trade, supply chains, and the global economy. This is why the U.S. must double down on its financial and political commitments to maintaining its blue-water superiority.

The South China Sea is one of the world's most hotly contested strategic locations. The critical role it plays as a key link in global maritime commerce cannot be underestimated. For two decades, China has been using the South China Sea as a stepping-off point to extend the reach of its military in the region. Under Xi Jinping's leadership, China has transparently used the People's Liberation Army Navy as the vehicle to assert its physical sovereignty over this strategic waterway. Why does China care so much?

THE STRATEGIC IMPORTANCE OF THE SOUTH CHINA SEA

To appreciate the strategic importance of the South China Sea today, think of the Rhine River in Central Europe as a parallel. Beginning in

Graubünden, Switzerland, and flowing 766 miles northbound through six European countries, the Rhine has long been a strategic economic and military link. Going back two thousand years, the Rhine represented the northernmost frontier separating the Roman Empire from what the Romans considered to be lands inhabited by barbarians. In a sense, the Rhine has always been a "superhighway" connecting Southern and Northern Europe. Since few roadways existed before Roman times, the Rhine for thousands of years was the only way to travel, a fact that led to its exploitation. During the Middle Ages and up to the 18th century, about 350 independent states in the region fought for survival by forcefully extracting taxes wherever they could. Often referred to as "robber barons," those Central European fiefdoms located on or near the Rhine would stretch massive chains across the Rhine River at its narrowest points. The robber barons then erected formidable castles that served as physical bulwarks to prevent merchants and their goods from traveling up and down the Rhine waterway. Their aim was simple—no watercraft was permitted passage without first paying a toll or tax to the local castle owner. This went on for over one thousand years along the Rhine until the practice stopped with the emergence of European nation-states in the 18th and 19th centuries.

One thing that hasn't changed in the last three thousand years is that the overwhelming majority of global trade is still dependent on the world's waterways and oceans. According to the United Nations Conference on Trade and Development (UNCTAD), more than 80 percent of global trade by volume and at least 70 percent by value is transported around the world by ships—container, dry bulk, wet bulk, and tankers of all sizes and types. Massive volumes of goods pass each day to and from Asia via the South China Sea. China is the largest global exporter in the region, producing trillions of dollars' worth of goods (or four times the value of exports out of South Korea and nearly eight times the value of exports out of Japan). No one is exactly sure how much trade passes through the South China

Sea, but a figure often quoted in public sources is $5 trillion per year. The South China Sea serves as the strategic conduit for Japan, South Korea, Taiwan, nations throughout Southeast Asia, and, of course, China as the largest user. The world's supply chains depend on it. Even today, China remains an export-driven economy, which is the principal reason why for over thirty-five years China's economic growth outpaced every other country in the world. Since over 60 percent of China's trade value goes by sea, free and open access to the South China Sea is absolutely critical for China in order to maintain its export dominance.

CHINA VERSUS THE U.S. PACIFIC FLEET

China has always resented the U.S. Navy maintaining a physical presence in the Asia Pacific region for more than two hundred years. The U.S. Navy's presence is possible because America maintains a string of strategic bases stretched across the Pacific, from the U.S. West Coast, to Hawaii, to the Marshall Islands, to Guam, and ultimately to Japan and Korea. The possibility of a U.S.-sponsored physical embargo of Chinese ports has worried Chinese military leaders since the end of the Korean War when China and the United States found themselves at odds. The choke point for any embargo of China would logically be centered around the South China Sea; hence China's obsession with asserting its sovereignty over this strategic passage.

Other than China's concerns about the U.S. presence in the region, the South China Sea is a hotly contested area for two reasons. First, the South China Sea borders on China, Vietnam, parts of Malaysia, the Philippines, Taiwan, and Brunei, with Korea and Japan located to the far north. Each of these countries has a legitimate economic and military interest in maintaining the South China Sea as a vital maritime route due to its strategic position from both a trade and a military standpoint. Of particular interest are the numerous small coral outcroppings and atolls that dot the South China Sea. Two are particularly sought-after—the Spratly Islands and the Paracel Islands. Since the end of World War II, governments throughout the region have engaged in continual disputes over which nations can claim sovereign rights over the South China Sea based on their proximity to these random reefs and outcroppings.

There is a second allure of the South China Sea that extends beyond serving as a strategic route for maritime carriers of global trade goods and resources. It is all about oil and natural gas. The South China Sea reached an even higher level of importance to the Chinese when, during the late 1960s, massive reserves of natural resources were discovered below its surface. According to the U.S. Energy Information Administration, the South China Sea may contain up to 14 trillion cubic feet of natural gas as well as 16 billion to 18 billion barrels of proven but unexploited oil reserves. In an energy-hungry world, claiming legal rights to these massive energy reserves has been an enormous incentive for countries throughout the region, and particularly for China, because its highly industrialized infrastructure cannot survive without assured supplies of oil and gas. Many countries have sought to claim ownership of the various islands and coral outcroppings throughout the South China Sea because of what lies beneath them.

THE PHILIPPINES VERSUS CHINA

The most high-profile and longest-running dispute over sovereignty in the South China Sea has been between the Philippines and China. After years of confrontations, everything came to a head in 1982 when the Philippines ratified the United Nations Convention on the Law of the Sea (UNCLOS). Declaring itself an "archipelagic state," it then took steps to legally declare its sovereign rights to the Spratly Islands and various coral reefs, since they lay within two hundred nautical miles of the Philippines' shoreline.[1]

The already frequent skirmishes between the Philippines and China reached a crisis point when Chinese frigates intercepted Filipino fishing boats in an area near the Philippines coast. At the same time, in July 2012, the Vietnamese National Assembly passed legislation declaring that the maritime borders of Vietnam included the Spratly and Paracel Islands, and that they thus belonged to Vietnam. The Philippine government upped the ante when it filed a formal claim with the Permanent Court of Arbitration under Annex VII to the Law of the Sea Treaty. The Philippine government demanded that the international arbitral tribunal once and for all invalidate claims asserted by China over vast areas in the South China Sea adjacent to the Philippines. In a dramatic decision, the Permanent Court of Arbitration in July 2016 ruled decisively against China by issuing a unanimous award in favor of the sovereignty claims of the Philippines. Not surprisingly, Beijing immediately and publicly rejected the tribunal's ruling. Since 2016, China has openly continued to erect extensive military enclaves and airfields on atolls throughout the South China Sea, continuing to assert its sovereignty over the region.

Commercial and military disputes continue to this day. China, because of its physical presence on the atolls, has created a zone that has the potential to interrupt maritime trade if China decides to do so. Over the last ten years the Chinese Navy has emerged as the second most powerful navy in the world, after only the United States. This means none of the nations located in Southeast Asia possess the military capacity (or political will) to challenge China's claims of sovereignty. The only counterpoint is when the omnipresent U.S. Navy vessels regularly patrol the region with the stated policy of keeping the sea lanes open for all countries. This becomes even more confrontational as China moves to exploit the vast oil and natural gas reserves that lie beneath the surface of the South China Sea.

THE SOUTH CHINA SEA AND CHINA'S GLOBAL REPUTATION

Xi Jinping is constantly promoting China as a leading global economic and military power while rejecting the claims of other nations to their rights within the South China Sea. At the same time, China is actively seeking to project its image as a responsible global leader. Those two ambitions directly conflict with each other. The dilemma Xi faces is that exerting influence over the South China Sea comes at a high price for what he sees as China's global image. There are five negative impacts on China's reputation.

First, for any serious country to be a respected global leader, it must maintain a positive reputation in its relationships with international organizations. This is why in 1995 China placed such a high premium on becoming a member of the World Trade Organization (WTO). With the strong backing of then-president Bill Clinton, and over the objections of some nations, China was admitted to the WTO. But with WTO membership comes the commitment to obey rules set down for members, and China for the first time pledged to cooperate. Now, though, having rejected a clear and unanimous decision by the world's highest arbitration tribunal on the rights of the Philippines in the South China Sea, it is difficult for China to argue that it will respect future international decisions that do not go in its favor.

Next, China is working hard to supplant the United States as a dominant economic force in Asia, particularly throughout Southeast Asia. Unfortunately, the door was opened wide for Xi Jinping when in 2017 President Donald Trump, after just a few weeks in office, rejected the United States' membership in the newly formed Trans-Pacific Partnership (TPP).[2] Now China is attempting to step into the role rejected by the U.S. as a member of the Regional Comprehensive Economic Partnership (RCEP). However, the Biden Administration is actively taking steps to renew its involvement in the Asian region. China's military potential in the South China Sea to interdict trade patterns makes it difficult for China at the same time to claim it is in favor of an open and free global trade system.

Third, with its growing military presence in the Spratly Islands and elsewhere throughout the South China Sea, China is now transparently signaling its intention to become increasingly militarily aggressive throughout the region. This raises concerns not just in the handful of countries bordering on the South China Sea but also as far away as India, which is now part of the "Quad" with the United States, Australia, and Japan.

Next, no one can seriously question that China today is a premier manufacturing center for many types of products, most of which are destined for buyers outside China. These products feed into the global supply chain and are shipped by maritime vessels to consumers and assemblers worldwide. China's growing military capability to block passage to the South China Sea, if it so desires, weakens China's appeal as a preferred place for European and North American companies to fulfill their contract manufacturing. Can European and American buyers reasonably rely on the South China Sea always being open? Consider how Russia's war with the Ukraine since February 2022 has impacted the global supply chain. Since China remains an export-driven economy, managing the balance between military might in the region and an export economy is increasingly difficult. There are already many leading American and European companies rethinking their traditional sourcing, realigning their manufacturing capabilities to out of China, or at least securing a second source outside China.[3]

Finally, China for a decade has actively pursued its Belt and Road Initiative, which is intended to make China fully integrated through various land and sea routes with the rest of the world. Countries that still depend on global trade by free and open sea routes will be less likely to embrace Belt and Road financing initiatives promoted by the Chinese. As a number of governments have learned to their dismay, failure to meet their repayment obligations to the Chinese has resulted in concessions such as "ninety-nine-year leases," which of course are slanted to benefit China.

In short, if China's success in the South China Sea is achieved by forcefully exerting its military and political influence, China will suffer unintended consequences—principally, damaging its export economy and risking the status of world leader that it covets.

IT'S TIME TO DOUBLE DOWN

Despite what China says in its ever-expanding charm offensive as a global power, it is determined to build its military presence as a counterweight to the United States throughout the Pacific. Anyone who doubts this only has to look at how China has militarized the South China Sea, creating the potential to block trade in the region if it so wishes. This is a bold economic and political challenge to countries in Southeast Asia, Japan, Korea, Taiwan, and even India.

The U.S. Navy for more than 230 years has consistently operated with the goal of keeping sea lanes open around the world. While the U.S. Navy has enforced international laws respecting the borders of countries with coastlines, China's response has been to rapidly build up its navy as an offensive force. Today, China's navy has more ships than the U.S. Navy. At current rates of construction, China's number of ships will increase significantly over the next ten years. However, China as of now has only two aircraft carrier groups, while the U.S. Navy has eleven. All of the U.S. Navy carriers are nuclear-driven, which isn't true for China's carriers. Also, the submarines under U.S. control far outnumber what China has, though the Chinese are rapidly working to catch up.

The bottom line is that the U.S. Congress and whichever political party controls the White House need to take China's military threat in the Pacific seriously. One significant challenge facing the U.S. Navy is that, while its overall resources in a qualitative sense are greater than China's, the United States spreads its naval resources all over the globe; it cannot focus only on the Pacific. This makes China's buildup in the Pacific a more immediate as opposed to long-term threat. The U.S. has maybe a decade at most to accelerate the growth of its naval forces before China has the capacity to go face-to-face throughout the Pacific region, thus forcing the U.S. to permanently assign more ships to the Pacific. At the same time, the U.S. Navy must continue to upgrade and expand the number of its bases spread throughout the Pacific, which will require significant additional appropriations and support from the U.S. Congress.

CHAPTER EIGHTEEN

FIGHT CYBER WITH CYBER

"Cyber" is a word that is difficult, if not impossible, to define. Cyber can refer to an object, a policy, or an idea. The word "cyber" can appear alone or in combination with words such as "attack," "sphere," or "space." Cyber is frequently linked with computers, information technology, metadata, and virtual reality. It is similarly found in conjunction with robotics, computerization, or spear-phishing. The uses of cyber vary greatly, and its impact can range from benign to threatening. In its most extreme form, cyber is the prefix of "warfare" in which cyber technologies are weaponized by individuals, companies, and governments in order to steal trade secrets, stealthily acquire valuable technologies, or illegally undermine competitors.

Not a day goes by without at least one news report of a malicious cyberattack. Cyberattacks, such as the June 2023 attack on New Zealand's parliament, can target government agencies, banks, telecom providers, personnel records, satellite communications, ballistic missile silos, government vendors, corporate finances, infrastructure assets—the list is endless. This has forced all nations to take cyber seriously.

While cyber in its illegal form is frequently used as the vehicle to ferret out valuable confidential information stored on computers, cyber's most serious damage occurs when employed covertly by foreign governments and their unofficial agents against perceived competitors or enemies. Governments, no matter where they are located, regularly engage in some form of cyber activity. To pretend otherwise would be naive. Government cyber activities can be divided into two camps—defensive or offensive. In their more benign form, governments undertake defensive cyber activities to protect their own national self-interests. One common action is when a government uses cyber tools to fend off attacks carried out by foreign agents acting surreptitiously (officially or unofficially) on behalf of a foreign government. A nation's leaders are grossly negligent if they fail to plan for and provide effective defensive barriers against cyberattacks that can target infrastructures such as electrical grids, water supplies, natural gas pipelines, military installations, and nuclear power plants. If a malicious attack does occur, cyber defenses must be in place to react swiftly and then respond in kind, if justified. This means governments must at a minimum erect adequate cyber resources to shield a country's economy and military from all forms of foreign and domestic interference. Take Israel, for example. Israel regularly employs both defensive and offensive cyber capabilities where it perceives its political enemies are most vulnerable. Another example is Iran, which regularly uses cyber offensively and, in the case of domestic dissent, can shut down web access during antigovernment protests.

The United States maintains its own offensive and defensive cyber capabilities. The U.S. Cybersecurity and Infrastructure Security Agency (CISA) identifies and, when appropriate, publishes information about threatened cyber activities by foreign governments and harmful actors targeting the United States. CISA is the sharp end of the stick for America. It closely coordinates its activities with the Federal Bureau of Investigation (FBI) and other government security divisions such as the U.S. Office of the Director of National Intelligence (ODNI).

HOW CHINA PLAYS IN THE CYBER WORLD

Much like Russia, North Korea, and Iran, the Chinese government for years has been engaged in offensive cyber activities. China recognized early on the power of cyber as a mechanism to both protect Chinese national interests and flex them globally. As early as 1991, as the original Gulf War was ending, the Chinese military foresaw the potential impact that modern technologies might be able to exert over China's perceived global competitors. In 2004, the Chinese military embraced the concept of "informatization,"[1] which would ultimately become a priority for enhancing the capabilities of China's armed forces.

China significantly stepped up its prioritization of cyber when Xi Jinping became China's leader in 2013. The strategic importance of cyber warfare was first publicly acknowledged by the Chinese in a 2013 study by China's Academy of Military Science (then known as the Science of Military Strategy), and then again in a paper released by China's Ministry of National Defense in 2015.

When Xi Jinping met with former president Barack Obama in 2015, the two leaders reportedly discussed the topic of commercial cyber espionage. According to published reports, the economic costs of commercial (nonmilitary) information stolen from American companies and related entities is between $300 billion and $600 billion annually. This amazing figure is in addition to the costs of cyberattacks directed at U.S. military and intelligence agencies. Following the 2015 meeting between Xi and Obama, there seemed to be some discernible drop in cyber warfare. However, that ended when Donald Trump became president of the United States in 2017, at which point the overall relationship between China and the U.S. became increasingly adversarial. Particularly following the Trump Administration's imposition of tariffs on China, U.S. entities such as CISA have tracked and identified increasing numbers of Chinese-sponsored attacks. The Biden Administration in July 2021 released a public statement suggesting that the People's Republic of China ordered an exploitation of a Microsoft Exchange server, carried out by four specifically identified Chinese cyber actors. It was then clear that China had accelerated its use of cyber beyond merely as a tool to acquire foreign technologies. Cyber became an offensive weapon for China to use against the West.

As China became increasingly aggressive in targeting critical infrastructure within the United States, President Biden responded by signing into law the Cyber Incident Reporting for Critical Infrastructure Act of 2022 (CIRCIA). In short, CIRCIA directed that CISA develop and implement regulations requiring private entities to report cyber incidents and ransomware payments. Prior to this new law, private and publicly traded companies were often reluctant to report cyberattacks, but such reports are critical to making the U.S. government aware of where attacks are happening so appropriate resources can be deployed and trends can be identified. It is expected that within twenty-four months after the enactment of CIRCIA, the reporting of cyber incidents will become mandatory.

U.S. government officials themselves have been targeted by Chinese hackers. It was reported in July 2023 that the emails of the U.S. Ambassador to Beijing, Robert Nicholas Burns, were the target of a Chinese-sanctioned cyberattack. The assistant secretary of state for East Asian and Pacific affairs, Daniel J. Kritenbrink, was also reportedly a target, as was Secretary of Commerce Gina Raimondo, who made an official visit to confer with Chinese leaders in late August 2023. While a U.S. State Department representative refused to share the scope of the incident, it is possible that hundreds of thousands of U.S. government email accounts were breached. All of this is why cyber must receive increased attention and priority by the U.S. government. CISA director Jen Easterly has in a number of public appearances stressed the importance of cybersecurity from the perspective of the United States. At a panel conference in Las Vegas in August 2023, she could not have been more clear when she laid out the challenge: "I hope that people are taking seriously a pretty stark warning about the potential for China to use their very formidable capabilities in the event of a conflict in the Taiwan Straits to go after our [the United States'] critical infrastructure."

This is not meant to be a comprehensive examination of the serious challenges posed by cyber (which would require expertise I lack).

Instead, my focus is on how China today is actively and continuously involved in targeting and exploiting weaknesses in federal, state, and local governments and in critical infrastructures throughout the United States as well as other nations. That is the reality. While there is no doubt that the U.S. and other Western countries are conducting their own cyber activities, at this point they appear to be primarily defensive in nature but do have the potential to become offensive. The dilemma for Xi Jinping and his advisors is to decide whether China's ongoing offensive use of cyber is consistent with its economic ambitions throughout Asia. As China becomes better known (and feared) for its overtly aggressive cyber espionage activities, can China reasonably expect the world's compliance and cooperation with its Belt and Road initiatives? The challenge China faces is that as it becomes increasingly aggressive in the cyber area, it weakens its attractiveness as a potential economic partner.

CHAPTER NINETEEN

CONTINUE TO OUT-INNOVATE CHINA

During a period of rising tensions between the United States and the Soviet Union, a headline on October 5, 1957, shocked America (see page 174). Russia was first to launch a satellite into Earth's orbit. The space race had begun in earnest.

In the following weeks, numerous editorial pages bemoaned America's failure to best the Soviets in technology. The fear was that the advanced Soviet technology would soon dominate the world both militarily and economically. Sputnik spurred America's resolve to win the race.

"We choose to go to the moon." On September 12, 1962, President John F. Kennedy upped the ante when he gave what is known as his "Moon Speech" at Rice University. The young president promised that America would be the first nation to land a man on the moon and would spend whatever was necessary to achieve that goal. On July 20, 1969, Neil Armstrong—an American—was the very first human to set foot on the surface of the moon.

The space race was about more than landing on the moon. It was about which country—the Soviet Union or the United States—possessed superior technologies. Which would best the other in terms of bigger and better technological achievements? The ultimate collapse of the Soviet Union in 1991 settled that question once and for all.

As dramatic as the space race was, an even more important race is now occurring, this time between the United States and China. The race is all about technological superiority. It is technology that will have the greatest impact on the global economy for the balance of this century. China has declared it intends to win this race, and it is long past time for the United States to wake up.

It is an amazing story, how China has reached this point. Between 1949 and 1980, China was one of the poorest countries on the planet. Its economy was impoverished, and millions of Chinese starved to death during the 1960s because the country could not feed its growing population. Prior to 1980, China engaged in a minuscule amount of international trade and lagged far behind the rest of the world technologically. Few products were being manufactured or exported by China because it lacked adequate capital, had a nonexistent infrastructure, and had no indigenous technologies. It was only after the death of Mao Zedong in 1976 that China's leadership realized that if China had any hope of growing its economy and feeding its people, it had to obtain access to technologies and vast sources of funding.

CHINA'S AMAZING THIRTY-YEAR INDUSTRIALIZATION

From 1980 through 2012, Deng Xiaoping and his successors focused their attention on building a highly efficient manufacturing base. The Chinese government underwrote and sustained the financing of state-owned enterprises and assisted smaller, more independent manufacturers at the provincial levels. During that period, China erected a massive infrastructure of roads, railroads, ports, airports, and the physical facilities necessary to support the output of an army of Chinese manufacturers, large and small. This growth spurt was accelerated by setting up special economic zones throughout China that acted as magnets for Chinese manufacturers, which were then tied into the infrastructure the Chinese government underwrote. For three decades, trillions of dollars in hard currencies—dollars, yen, euros, pounds, and won—flowed into China. What further empowered Chinese companies was when Western countries saw the opportunity to manufacture their products more inexpensively in China than at home. By 2010, China had experienced one of the most explosive periods of economic growth in the history of the world. There were some years when the Chinese economy grew 10 to 12 percent.[1] Even during the global financial crisis of 2007 to 2009, China's economy responded well. Around 2012, it became clear that China had achieved global dominance in low- to mid-level manufacturing. But while many countries would have been delighted to achieve such strong levels of economic growth, China was still not satisfied.

WHY CHINA HUNGERS FOR ITS OWN TECHNOLOGICAL BASE

After three decades of welcoming massive inbound investment that enabled the development of its manufacturing base, China became frustrated. This feeling coincided with Xi Jinping emerging as China's leader in 2013. Though China was an acknowledged manufacturing center of the world, Xi realized that many of the companies driving China's economy were foreign, not Chinese. With some exceptions, foreign companies such as Apple and a multitude of other American and European firms were using China and its inexpensive labor as their base to meet the demands of a global market. Thus many of the profits benefited the Western companies, not the Chinese manufacturers. Xi Jinping and his Chinese Communist Party colleagues were determined to have Chinese companies dominate this market, rather than depend on foreign companies and consumers for income. A related reason is that foreign companies were manufacturing in China and paying back very little to the Chinese government. As profits continued to grow for foreign companies, those profits were flowing out of China and into the reserves of their own countries.

Also frustrating the Chinese was the feeling that that they were not receiving enough manufacturing contracts for high-technology items. An example of this was, and still is, microchips. The few Chinese companies that were actually manufacturing these specialized products were being forced to pay royalties to technology holders that were not Chinese.

Yet another factor simultaneously working against China's interests was that Chinese labor, while very inexpensive and widely available in the 1980s and 1990s, was becoming increasingly costly. In other words, Chinese labor was no longer "cheap." Part of this labor issue resulted from the role played by China's currency, the renminbi. The renminbi, while tied to the dollar, was forcing the costs of Chinese labor higher versus the international marketplace. The only answer was for China to slowly but surely shift its manufacturing base toward producing more sophisticated and technologically advanced products. To accomplish this, China needed to acquire its own technologies.

It was then that Xi Jinping decided that it was critical for manufacturers in China to use Chinese-developed technologies. His goal was (and still is) to ultimately break free of Western dependence. Xi concluded that Chinese industry would no longer be solely dependent on Western technology if it could build its own technology base. Therefore, China began to pursue policies focusing on a "two-technology" approach.

ARE WE HEADED TOWARD A TWO-TECHNOLOGY WORLD?

There was no easy way to achieve this ambitious goal outright, but China did have some options. After Xi Jinping came into power, Chinese companies were encouraged to go around the globe seeking out technologies to acquire. This often took the form of buying interests in foreign companies or joint-venturing with them so that Chinese companies could gain access to higher levels of Western technology. Simultaneously, China funded and directed increased R&D in Chinese companies in those areas that China predicted would have great future potential. One example of such a targeted area was artificial intelligence (AI), which turned out to be a smart bet for the Chinese, as recently AI has grown explosively. There are also numerous reports of China's security agencies stealing foreign technologies.

Next, China began increasing pressure on foreign companies that were located in or conducting business in China. China adopted policies, directly and indirectly, to "encourage" foreign companies to share their technology with Chinese companies. Often this meant forming joint ventures in which technology rights would be transferred to the Chinese. Because of the power held by SOEs in China, these SOEs could exert enormous leverage to force foreign partners to transfer their technologies into China. Then there were ongoing efforts by Chinese security agencies through the use of cyber to steal foreign technologies.

MADE IN CHINA 2025

If there was any question that Xi Jinping and the CCP had drastically changed course, it became clear in 2015 with the announcement of Made in China 2025—China's national industrial and strategic plan. Intending to further accelerate China's manufacturing capacities, Made in China 2025 aimed to source as many products as possible from China and to strengthen the capacity of Chinese suppliers. While China would continue to use its current technology and exporting capacities, the overall goal was to exponentially upgrade the ability of Chinese industries to thrust China forward as a powerhouse in the technology field.

In getting to this point, China had already devoted significant resources to predict what technology sectors would be most valuable in the future. When the Made in China 2025 initiative was announced, the Chinese identified the following key industries: robotics, biotech, aerospace, smart manufacturing (3D printing), maritime engineering, electric vehicles, new materials, agricultural machinery and equipment, advanced rail, and pharmaceuticals. Within these sectors, particular attention was paid to AI and machine learning, the Internet of Things (IoT), and, as an attempt to help the Chinese economy, electric vehicles and green energy.

China then focused its attention on leading Chinese companies such as Huawei (telecommunications and electronics), Baidu (autonomous vehicles and artificial intelligence), Alibaba Group (e-commerce), and several dozen others. The charge—not an option—given to leaders of those Chinese companies was to aggressively take the reins in developing their own technologies and using them to heighten the quality of Chinese manufacturing. No one knows how much the Chinese government has spent to date in promoting these industrial sectors, but without question it is a multibillion-dollar effort in the form of direct state funding and subsidies such as low-interest loans and tax breaks.

Since 2015, China has achieved significant advancements in a number of key targeted industries. One such advancement was on grand display during the opening ceremonies of the 2022 Beijing Winter Olympics, with its amazing show of cutting-edge drone technology.[2] Similarly, the Chinese have also made significant strides in surveillance and facial recognition technologies, which have been used as a way for the Chinese leadership to observe and control everything going on in China. While not widely publicized, AI is another area that has moved forward since the Made in China 2025 policy was implemented. Digitizing the economy will continue to advance in China. One of the most significant areas of advancement in China involves 5G communications. The use of 5G along with the massive data collection capabilities of Chinese companies has pushed those technologies forward to the point that in some cases China is now a world leader.

WESTERN INNOVATION CONTINUES

While this has been going on in China, the United States and other Western countries have continued aggressively pushing forward with their own innovations. Although it is a rough calculation, it appears that about two-thirds of global technologies are Western-based, as opposed to one-third from China. China, obviously, intends to reverse this ratio to its favor. You might wonder why the U.S. in particular has been so successful in technological innovation. There is not one single reason, but rather a combination of factors. Without a doubt, some American technologies that have been successfully commercialized are a result of military R&D spinoffs. Back in the 1960s, America's efforts to put a man on the moon led to numerous commercial applications that have directly benefited the U.S. and other Western countries. In addition, the U.S. government continues to fund basic and sometimes applied research in leading academic centers throughout the country. The U.S. government has opened up opportunities for private companies to form joint ventures with governmental departments and branches. Of course, there continues a long tradition of targeted research by government organizations such as the Defense Advanced Research Projects Agency (DARPA). While the U.S. remains the global leader in the design of advanced semiconductor development, retaining its position is by no means guaranteed.[3] China continues to expend resources trying to create its own technologies for the application of semiconductors. Whether China's infrastructure, with its government-dominated watch over technological development, will prevail is not certain. Clearly China, because of its basic structure, is unable to copy the U.S. model, and instead it must come up with its own.

PROSPECTS FOR A TWO-TECHNOLOGY WORLD

If China had its choice, it would obviously want Chinese technologies to become the sole platform for many of the products and technologies utilized in order to expand its economic and diplomatic reach. Part of this can be tied into China's extremely ambitious Belt and Road Initiative. The Belt and Road Initiative, which was undertaken in 2013, was and remains the largest infrastructure project in the history of the world. Basically, China's goal is to link more than sixty countries in Asia, Africa, and Europe together through a series of roads, ports, and railroads so that those countries would be intimately connected—and some might say controlled—by their relationship with China.

While the United States and Western countries currently still have a lead in technology development and implementation, they would be foolish not to take seriously the massive efforts by China to promote its own technologies. At this point, it is impossible to predict whether China will succeed. One serious barrier to its goals is the internet. Because the internet essentially began through military-focused research and experimentation done in the United States and the United Kingdom, English became the dominant language used on the network. At least 400 million people are native English speakers, and a roughly equal number speak English as a second language. English has been adopted by more websites than any other language. The dominant presence of English on the internet continues to make it difficult for China to establish a presence of its own.

While Western-based technologies still dominate the global economy, it is clear that China will do all it can to reverse this trend. It will be interesting to see how this develops over the next decade. This MaxTrend® is a truly critical challenge that the United States and its Western allies need to confront head-on. If they don't, the future for the West is dim.

CHAPTER TWENTY

INVEST IN AFRICA AND ITS RESOURCES

Africa never ceases to surprise and confound. Take Kenya, for example. When I visited Nairobi National Park (and you certainly should as well), I was amazed by the zebras, lions, giraffes, elephants, and particularly rhinos roaming freely throughout the grounds. While there, you feel like you are thousands of miles away from the cosmopolitan world. But if you look just to the north, you can see in the distance the dramatic skyline of Kenya's capital city of Nairobi. Nairobi, the largest city in a country of 55 million people, is less than ten miles away from this awe-inspiring wildlife preserve. The juxtaposition of Nairobi, home to more than one thousand international companies and thousands more Kenyan companies, with the wildlife so close by is difficult to comprehend.

At all levels—diplomatic, commercial, private, and governmental—investing throughout Africa must become a higher priority for the United States. Why? Because while the United States has basically been ignoring Africa's massive potential, China has not. Chinese construction and mining companies have over the last decade captured major infrastructure projects and access to strategic rare metals because of China's aggressive investment strategy targeting African nations. Greater attention from the U.S. to Africa can help to offset China's current advantage. Africa possesses two key attractions: (1) abundant national resources; and (2) a young and increasingly educated workforce. To put it bluntly, Africa could very likely emerge as a counterpoint to China as a global manufacturing center.

Despite its size and potential, Africa is not as globally appreciated as it deserves to be. Made up of fifty-four countries, one disputed territory, and three dependencies (according to the UN Statistics Division), Africa is divided into five regions: Northern Africa, Western Africa, Central (or Middle) Africa, East Africa, and Southern Africa. Each region contains countries with their own unique languages, cultures, and challenges. Throughout Africa lie vast deposits of mineral wealth. Sadly, for centuries, those natural resources were exploited by nations and trading companies from around the world. The exploitation of mineral wealth has come at a tragic price for Africa's people and its ecosystem, because exploitation nurtures corruption.

Unfortunately, aside from its mineral wealth, history, and fascinating culture, Africa suffers from an overall poor international reputation. Wars and conflicts that have led to tragic levels of starvation among Africa's poorest regularly dominate headlines. Throw in wildlife poaching, kidnappings, pandemics, and financial scams, and what ends up in the news drives a negative and undeserved narrative about Africa and its capabilities.

Climate change also poses significant challenges for Africa. Because of its size and location on the planet, global warming impacts Africa more than any other continent. With a large agricultural sector made up of primarily small, inefficient plots of arable land, producing enough food to feed its populace has always been a challenge in Africa. Now climate change has made the situation even worse. The one bright spot is that most of Africa still has sufficient rainfall, which is not the case in other parts of the world. But these factors do not tell the whole story. There are other trends that promise better times for Africa in the future.

The most striking and optimistic fact about Africa is that in less than twenty years, it will have a larger population than China. By 2050, Africa could be responsible for 25 percent of the world's total population. Africa by the second half of the 21st century will have the potential to compete with and potentially best China in terms of demographics and a viable labor force. This has not been lost on the Chinese.

For decades China has strategically expanded its reach around the world, and one of its major targets has been Africa and its as of yet untapped potential. As part of its Belt and Road Initiative, China has worked hard to forge closer ties with African nations, particularly those nations that possess natural resources such as rare metals that China must have in order to maintain its manufacturing edge. Part of Beijing's strategy has been to lend money to African nations to construct much-needed railways, roads, dams, ports, and other infrastructure projects.

Following are three examples of how China is aggressively pursuing investments and seeking out increasingly valuable natural resources throughout Africa.

- China's Zijin Mining Group, which has been snapping up lithium deposits in South America for years, is now trying to gain control over one of the world's largest hard rock deposits of lithium located in the Democratic Republic of the Congo.
- According to published reports, Chinese firms (including Chengxin Lithium Group, Yahua Group, Canmax Technologies, Sinomine Resource Group, and Zhejiang Huayou Cobalt) have invested more than $1 billion to pursue projects in Zimbabwe.
- China's Panyu Chu Kong Steel Pipe Co. was awarded a major contract to supply and deliver pipes to the Port of Tanga in Tanzania for the massive East African Crude Oil Pipeline. The project is being backed by China's National Offshore Oil Corporation (CNOOC), one of its largest state-owned enterprises.

THE UNITED STATES AND AFRICA

Africa today does not occupy as high a priority in U.S. foreign policy as it should. This has been true for the Biden Administration, the Trump Administration, and even the Obama Administration.[1] In fact, the last president to pay any real attention to Africa was former president George W. Bush. Because the Bush Administration's highly criticized invasion of Iraq and its Middle East policies consumed most of the nation's attention, President Bush's personal interest and investment in Africa never received any genuine public interest. Only recently have Bush's initiatives gained some much-belated attention. Surprising as it may seem, if any American president is truly appreciated in Africa today, it is George W. Bush.

Alarmed by the AIDS crisis that ran rampant throughout the African continent, President Bush in 2003 asked the U.S. Congress to approve and fund the President's Emergency Plan for AIDS Relief (PEPFAR). Since then, the United States has contributed more than $100 billion to provide AIDS relief in Africa where it is most prevalent.[2] The stated goal of PEPFAR was to ultimately eliminate HIV/AIDS (which today still infects more than 1.7 million people) by the year 2030. So far, the measurable success of the PEPFAR program has been impressive. According to experts, more than 25 million lives in Africa have benefited. About 75 percent of the individuals who contracted HIV are now receiving some form of treatment. The success of the Bush Administration's PEPFAR program should not be underestimated. I mention this not to single out President Bush and his humanitarian efforts, but to explain why the United States is viewed favorably among many nations throughout Africa.

The challenge for America now is to recognize that China has aggressively targeted Africa as a major place to invest and conduct business, and to understand why this is important. The clock is ticking, and the longer the United States fails to engage with Africa more fully, the wider the door opens for China to move many of Africa's fifty-four nations into the Chinese orbit. The U.S. has an already-established "in" with Africa and a base of goodwill. Ignoring that opportunity and handing the advantage to China would be short-sighted and ultimately damaging to America's reputation. There are four things America can do to immediately counterbalance China's influence in Africa.

- The U.S. government needs to aggressively upgrade both the quantity and quality of State Department personnel assigned to U.S. embassies and nongovernmental organizations (NGOs) throughout Africa. Key placement of representatives can help to open doors for American interests including U.S. companies seeking to do business in Africa.
- Africa harbors a vast trove of valuable natural resources. Rare earth elements essential to many highly advanced technologies are just one example. American companies with the support of the U.S. government need to foster meaningful partnerships with African countries that have desirable reserves and business opportunities.
- America needs to upgrade its efforts to provide financial assistance and grants to combat serious health crises throughout Africa as it did with the PEPFAR project. This is a tangible way to help Africa deal with real-life challenges while raising a positive profile of America throughout the African continent.
- At the highest diplomatic levels, America must devote significant efforts toward calling public attention to Africa's potential. At a minimum this should include regular presidential visits to Africa and the hosting of African leaders in Washington DC on a periodic basis.

CHAPTER TWENTY-ONE

EMBRACE INTERNATIONAL ORGANIZATIONS

During the Great Depression of the 1930s, the global economy completely collapsed. Back then there were no international organizations capable of bringing countries together in times of crisis. Following World War II, international organizations such as the World Trade Organization, the International Monetary Fund, and the United Nations were created and given the power to unite countries for the common good, providing certain rules are followed. China since 1949 has taken full advantage of what multilateral organizations have to offer, but only when it directly benefits China. The United States needs to fully reengage with international organizations in order to prevent the world from devolving into regional trading blocs. China must then either agree to fully participate or be pushed aside.

Across the world, a battle is being waged between the role played by international organizations and a growing countertrend favoring deglobalization. Will international organizations remain influential going forward, or will national governments increasingly adopt a go-it-alone approach? In my view, the answer will largely depend on which side of the battle China chooses. In short, China's dilemma is whether it will (1) decide to participate seriously as a responsible global leader by actively supporting international organizations; or (2) elect to go its own way as a military and economic colossus, creating its own unique bloc.

WHAT IS AN INTERNATIONAL ORGANIZATION?

International organizations are a relatively recent development in world governance. They first appeared in very limited numbers during the late 19th and early 20th centuries. Following the devastation wrought by World War I, there were some half-hearted attempts to bring countries together (such as the League of Nations), but most efforts were unsuccessful. It was only following World War II, when most of the world lay in ruins, that countries realized they had no choice but to join together and rebuild or face the grim prospects of a shattered world economy. While there is no precise definition of what an international organization is, basically it occurs when three or more national governments cooperate under a common set of rules or norms. Although the exact number is unclear, about three hundred international (or intergovernmental) organizations exist in 2024.

THE UNITED NATIONS

The best-known and largest international organization is the United Nations (UN). Established in October 1945, currently 192 countries and territories are official members of the United Nations. Other than the United Nations Assembly itself, there are roughly thirty organizations that fall under the UN umbrella. The mission of the UN and its related arms is to pursue international security and peace by encouraging nations of the world to cooperate more closely. When conflicts inevitably arise, the hope is that they are resolved in a peaceful manner. This makes the UN the most powerful intergovernmental organization in the world. Aside from its headquarters in New York, the UN and its affiliates maintain offices in Geneva, Nairobi, The Hague, Vienna, and several other locations.

Along with the goal of preventing wars and conflicts, the United Nations focuses much of its efforts on promoting global social welfare, which casts quite a wide net. One of the best-known UN affiliates is the World Health Organization (WHO), which is headquartered in Geneva and tasked with making healthcare an international priority. While generally respected, the WHO did encounter some controversy early in the COVID-19 crisis due to its reluctance to publicly release information about the source of the virus and China's level of involvement. The Food and Agricultural Organization and the International Fund for Agricultural Development each focus on health and agriculture. Another key organization under the United Nations is the Office of the High Commissioner for Human Rights, which promotes and acts to protect human rights, as do the International Rescue Committee (IRC) and the Office of the United Nations High Commissioner for Refugees (UNHCR). Other notable UN agencies actively deal with the environment, industrial development, international labor issues, aviation, and maritime disputes.

BEYOND THE UNITED NATIONS

While the United Nations and its affiliates are widely respected, other international organizations are equally influential in addressing global economic and political issues. Perhaps the best known is the European Union, along with others such as the Arab League (formerly the League of Arab States), ASEAN (the Association of Southeast Asian Nations), COMESA (the Common Market for Eastern and Southern Africa), CAN (the Andean Community), and the Commonwealth of Nations. Then there are those international organizations that focus primarily on economic issues, the largest and best known being the World Trade Organization (WTO) that is located in Geneva. The WTO is tasked with setting the rules for international trade and commerce. The Organization of American States, the Organisation for Economic Co-operation and Development, the World Bank, and a dozen or so others also seek to promote regional cooperation by focusing on economic development and investment opportunities.

GLOBAL FINANCE

Furthermore, there are international organizations that deal primarily with global financial matters, the most prominent being the International Monetary Fund (IMF). Formed at the end of World War II, the IMF continues to exert an enormous impact on international trade and business activities. Others active in global finance are the Asian Development Bank, the African Development Bank, the Inter-American Development Bank, the Islamic Development Bank, the European Central Bank, and the Caribbean Development Bank. Finally, there are important international organizations that do not necessarily fit neatly into a specific category, such as the Red Cross, the Organisation for the Prohibition of Chemical Weapons, the Organization of the Petroleum Exporting Countries, and international sports organizations (the most prominent being the International Olympic Committee).

The point of this lengthy list is to highlight how successful some international organizations have been with their global reach and positive influence over global growth for over a half century. Successes are possible because when countries agree to work closely together, great things can be accomplished. One example occurred when, during the global financial crisis (2007 to 2009), international organizations such as the International Monetary Fund stepped in and helped financially damaged countries recover by providing access to long-term, low-interest loans. Based on this history of assistance, one might assume that the nations of the world would want to keep these international organizations operating and enabling global cooperation, but that has not always been clear.

DEGLOBALIZATION IS BACK

A rapidly emerging movement counteracting the role of international organizations is aptly named "deglobalization." In short, deglobalization is the decision by some countries and political parties to deliberately back away from global cooperation and integration. While during the last fifty years there has been a preference toward international organizations, exceptions arose when countries became increasingly concerned about their own welfare and questioned (or in some cases ignored) the advice and directives of international organizations. One of the longest periods of deglobalization occurred during the 1930s; this was likely a reason why the Great Depression continued for so long. Many economists believe the Great Depression would have gone on much longer if not for the outbreak of World War II.

Deglobalization is more than just an economic issue. Deglobalization is often embraced by those nations looking to preserve what they perceive as their own unique social and cultural attributes. There are also technological drivers favoring deglobalization whereby nations desire to maintain control over their homegrown innovations and technologies. Other impacts of deglobalization include an increased focus on national income or capital, exports and imports of goods and services as a proportion of national income, costs of labor and migration rates, and whether foreign direct investment is expanding outward or growing more internalized.

The deglobalization mindset has become increasingly widespread since 2015. Perhaps the best example was the narrow decision by voters in Britain to leave the European Union under "Brexit." Although the negotiations surrounding the terms of the withdrawal took years, in the end the United Kingdom is no longer part of the European Union. Another trend of deglobalization was triggered by former president Donald Trump with his "America First" campaign platform and his open questioning of the value to the United States of international relationships and organizations such as NATO. Trump later imposed tariffs on China to offset a more than $300 billion trade deficit. The rise in deglobalization is directly tied to the MaxTrend® of rising nationalism described earlier. By their nature, nation-states are inward-looking and suspicious of globalization.

CHINA'S DILEMMA: DEGLOBALIZATION VERSUS MULTILATERALISM

Being part of an interconnected global economy has clear benefits and often less obvious drawbacks. None of us can predict with any real certainty where the global economy is headed. Will it continue as it has been, for better or for worse, since 1945? Will there be a global economy, or should we expect the world to become less interconnected? This is the dilemma now facing China's leadership under Xi Jinping. On its face, China should absolutely want to promote the presence and involvement of international organizations. The reason is because, over the last thirty-five years, China's annual GDP has increased astronomically largely due to its open trading system. China's phenomenal growth record by any measure could not have occurred without global organizations, and China aggressively took advantage of them. As noted several times throughout this book, China at the end of the Cultural Revolution in the mid-1970s found itself an exceptionally poor and backward country. Tens of millions of Chinese people suffered from malnutrition, and China's GDP, despite its large population, tended to be half that of other Asian nations at the time. Things only began to change after Deng Xiaoping kicked off China's transformation by introducing economic reforms that led to a total revamp of the Chinese economy. Over the next forty years, 800 million Chinese found themselves lifted out of poverty. By any calculation, this was an extraordinary accomplishment.

What truly kick-started China's economic growth? It happened after China became a member of the World Trade Organization in December 2001.[1] By 2002, 144 nations were WTO members, but China's entry was by no means preordained. Some nations had vigorously opposed China's entry because they feared China would over time become too dominant a force. In fact, that is exactly what happened after 2002, when the U.S. House of Representatives normalized trade relations with China. It was former president Bill Clinton who had advocated China's admission to the WTO, arguing that normalizing trade relations with China would result in political and economic benefits to both countries.[2] China's decision to join the WTO was driven by its desire to hold a formal position in global trade as well as to quickly improve the standard of living for the poorest Chinese, both of which occurred. One of the terms imposed by the WTO was that China had to agree to guarantee greater intellectual property protection to all WTO members and particularly to protect advanced technologies from Europe and the United States from theft. Under WTO urging, China also opened up its service sector in a number of important ways, directly benefiting parts of the U.S. economy that were providing services on a global basis and wanted to enter the growing Chinese economy.

Under the WTO, China benefited greatly by having increased access to the United States and other global markets. The volume of Chinese imports to the United States and Europe expanded rapidly after China joined the WTO. The U.S. consumer benefited greatly from the lower prices on a wide variety of consumer goods because they were made in China with less expensive labor. This, of course, led to an increase in Chinese manufacturing capacity. While America's manufacturing capacity diminished at the same time China's was growing, in the short run many American companies benefited from greater access to China.

With all of these factors, it would be logical and inescapable to assume that China would embrace the WTO and other international organizations, but that is not what happened. Now that China holds a dominant position within the WTO, it is better able to moderate or otherwise blunt claims that are brought by other WTO members. And with China's growing role within the WTO, the ability of the WTO to manage global trade has diminished.

As China aggressively promotes its Belt and Road Initiative, being a WTO member is no longer as important to China as it was when it was lifting itself out of poverty. China's economy is now the second largest in the world, and it wants to develop its own technologies and thus no longer be dependent on licensing, purchasing, or otherwise acquiring Western technologies. As a means to this end, China has made entry by foreign manufacturers or investors much more difficult than in the past. For those companies already operating in China, the Chinese government has used its power both directly and indirectly to "encourage" (force) joint ventures between Chinese and Western companies as well as the disclosure of confidential information and trade secrets to which China would not necessarily have access. China is also a member of other major international economic organizations such as the International Monetary Fund and the New Development Bank (formerly known as the BRICS Development Bank). While membership in those organizations comes with benefits, it also tends to make China's methods of aggressive economic expansion more difficult to execute.

SUPPORT INTERNATIONAL GROUPS
AND HOPE CHINA FOLLOWS

The time is coming when China will face a stark choice: either (1) embrace an interdependent world governed by international organizations; or (2) go in its own direction. With the one-hundred-year anniversary of the Chinese Communist Party coming up in 2049, China finds itself moving closer and closer to the time it has targeted to reach its goal of being the world's most powerful economic, military, and diplomatic country. The extent to which China elects to lessen or fully pull back from its membership in international organizations will directly affect when and how other world nations, which depend on these international organizations, might move in a different direction. The United States and its allies need to aggressively promote involvement in and the continued support of international organizations. It was an encouraging sign when the United States on July 11, 2023, officially rejoined the United Nations Educational, Scientific and Cultural Organization (UNESCO). This reversed a decision by the Trump Administration to withdraw from UNESCO in 2017, and the U.S. promised to pay its back dues of $619 million. This demonstration of the U.S. turning toward internationalism appears to be an effort to counter Chinese activism in some international organizations. The next five years will be critical in determining whether international organizations promoting a global trading system will continue to play an important role or will slowly fade into obscurity.

CHAPTER TWENTY-TWO

MAKE CHINA AMERICA'S HIGHEST PRIORITY

History doesn't repeat itself, but it often rhymes.
                              —Attributed to Mark Twain[1]

China today is America's most significant rival. This is nothing new; America has always had at least one major rival at one time or another. Only for the four years following World War II did America go unchallenged as the sole global military and economic power. That ended when the former USSR successfully tested a nuclear device on August 29, 1949, which triggered its Cold War with the United States. The Cold War continued until December 1991, when the Soviet Union officially collapsed with the resignation of Mikhail Gorbachev as its president.

Another rivalry emerged in the late 1970s when Japan began to economically challenge the United States. This became a public issue when Harvard professor Ezra F. Vogel published his 1979 book *Japan as Number One: Lessons for America*. Vogel predicted that Japan would soon overcome the United States as the world's largest economic power. Vogel's book was a bestseller in America, and a year or so later it sold more than half a million copies in Japan. The Japanese were both surprised and pleased by what Vogel prophesied. In fact, Vogel's book was embraced by many Japanese who were unhappy with Japan's status since the end of World War II. America's prominent influence was resented throughout Japan. One example is Japan's constitution that was largely drafted under the direction of General Douglas MacArthur, who lived in Japan for seven years following World War II. People today might only remember General MacArthur from the famous and carefully staged photograph of him striding onto the beach "reclaiming" the Philippines after Japan's occupation, but the pivotal role he played in transforming Japan into an economic and political powerhouse cannot be underestimated.

The predictions in Ezra Vogel's book were picked up by leading Japanese right-wing politician Shintaro Ishihara. Ishihara later became the governor of Tokyo for thirteen years, and in 1989 he published his own book titled *The Japan That Can Say No: Why Japan Will Be First among Equals*. It's no coincidence that Ezra Vogel wrote a foreword to Ishihara's book. With a collection of essays, one of which was penned by the brilliant Akio Morita of Sony, Ishihara challenged the United States and its global position at the time. While much of what Ishihara prophesied has since been discredited, it does prove how a single book can exert an enormous influence on national attitudes. During the late 1980s, the term "Japan bashing" became a popular accusation in Japan whenever a U.S. politician or public official made a statement or acted in a way the Japanese felt was inaccurate or unfavorable. One theory behind Ishihara's book was that the unique Japanese style of management was so superior to that of the U.S. that it guaranteed Japan's success.

THE JAPAN PARALLEL

Japan offers an interesting parallel to today's China in a number of ways. During the two decades following World War II, Japan went from being a devastated country to becoming the second largest economy in the world. How did Japan accomplish this? The Japanese decided to fund a manufacturing powerhouse (under the direction of Japan's Ministry of International Trade and Industry) that would, on a very carefully planned basis, push Japan forward in specific industries. It began in the early 1970s with the steel industry, in which Japan became one of the world's leaders. Later came Japanese-manufactured automobiles and, of course, electronics. Japanese innovators such as Akio Morita made Japan the envy of the world in its development and sale of electronic products. Even today, Sony, the brainchild of Akio Morita, continues to have a global presence as well as other major Japanese companies such as Mitsui, Mitsubishi, and Sumitomo.

This meant Japan had to rapidly move away from the poor reputation it had during the 1960s—that is, if it was "Made in Japan," it was shoddy. Japanese cars in the 1960s were essentially a joke. Less than two decades later, the Japanese reversed that impression. Into the mid-1980s, things seemed to be going swimmingly for Japan. Beginning in 1986, Japan entered its "bubble period," which continued until the early 1990s. Back then the Japanese economy was growing between 6 and 12 percent during certain periods, much as China's economy grew later. At its height, seven of the ten largest banks in the world were Japanese-owned, and the predictions of Ezra Vogel about Japan rising to the top appeared to be unnervingly accurate.

That all fell apart when the Japanese banking system changed. Prior to the 1980s, Japanese banks paid very little, if any, interest to their depositors. Beginning in the mid-1980s, as the Japanese banks expanded, the banks rich with the vast deposits of Japanese workers lent out money not just in Japan but globally. For a while, this drove up the value of Japanese bank stocks as well as the value of assets throughout Japan. The part of Japan's economy that was most directly impacted was real estate. Before the "bubble" burst in the early 1990s, real estate in Japan was valued higher than anywhere else in the world. In fact, at one point someone calculated that the land under the Imperial Palace in Tokyo, home to the emperor's family and surrounded by five kilometers of walking paths, was more valuable than all of the land in California.

Obviously, today this seems ridiculous, but back then, considering real estate values in Japan, many thought it made sense. The Japanese stock market (the Nikkei) continued to skyrocket as individuals borrowed money against appreciated real estate values and bought more stocks and more real estate if they could afford it. At its height, the Nikkei exceeded 30,000. When the crash ultimately came, the Nikkei plummeted, and it was only in 2023—after more than thirty years—that it once again reached those levels. Japan's economy experienced decades of deflation and great dislocations. The point is that if Vogel had been right, today Japan would be controlling the world. Instead, Japan fell into the doldrums and has only recently recovered.

CHINA IN 2024

This history of Japan and the (alleged) quote from Mark Twain, "History doesn't repeat itself, but it often rhymes," are relevant when you consider today's China. Parallels exist. As Deng Xiaoping was faced with a failed Chinese economy after the death of Mao, he, like the Japanese, decided that the best way for China to move forward was to establish a significant manufacturing base. Deng truly succeeded by placing China on a path so that, over the next three decades, it kept doubling the size of its economy until it ultimately bypassed Japan and became the second most powerful economy in the world. However, much of China's growth was dependent on its highly skilled and inexpensive workforce. Over the last decade the Chinese have discovered what the rest of the world already knew—when you have extensive manufacturing capabilities, eventually labor costs that were once inexpensive no longer are. On top of rising labor costs, China's demographics reveal rapidly diminishing numbers of Chinese laborers due to an aging workforce.

Another interesting parallel between Japan and China is that the Chinese early on recognized the importance of technology, not just in supporting their manufacturing base, but as a way to further their economy. When Xi Jinping became the undisputed leader of China in 2013, he more so than his predecessors resented that China was highly dependent on Western, not Chinese, technologies. As a result, China has made many attempts to promote its own brand of technologies, including the Made in China 2025 initiative. Xi Jinping used that as a stepping stone to target twenty-five key technologies that he saw as essential for China's future growth.

As China's exports grew through 2014–2015, it ran up significant trade imbalances with the United States. Basically, for every one dollar in goods that the U.S. sold to China, the Chinese would sell the Americans at least three times as much. The trade deficits grew rapidly out of balance during the Bush and Obama Administrations. One major consequence of China's growth for the U.S. economy was how badly America's domestic manufacturing capabilities were diminished. Today, manufacturing in the U.S. contributes about $2.3 trillion to its gross domestic product and employs about 12 million Americans. However, over the past twenty-five years, the U.S. lost more than seven million manufacturing jobs, most of which were outsourced to China by American companies seeking less expensive locations to manufacture consumer goods. The tragedy was that these were not just seven million jobs lost, but the workers who suffered the most were often minorities or individuals without college educations. They in essence became a "lost generation" of Americans who saw their jobs permanently outsourced overseas. After a time, their story became a platform of American politics.

It is only recently that American politicians—both Republicans and Democrats—have acknowledged the savage impact this has had on the U.S. economy. Since the Biden Administration took office in 2021, the U.S. government has begun to change its policies and is aggressively attempting to bring back American jobs that had gone to China. That is good for the United States and bad for China. The bottom line is that the Chinese economy cannot forever absorb the anticipated drop in overall demand. While it is unrealistic to expect that all of the manu-facturing for export purposes in China will disappear, expect Chinese capabilities to decline increasingly over time. Part of this is a direct result of the higher wages now demanded by laborers in China. Per-haps most difficult for the Chinese to accept will be the fact that R&D now being conducted in China will leave along with manufacturing jobs. Already companies around the world are reacting to the Chinese government's increased oversight of foreign operations in China. Those companies are disincentivized to stay or increase their presence there. This, along with the growing economic and military tensions between the U.S. and China, will discourage further outsourcing to China from the U.S. and the West.

MAKE CHINA AMERICA'S HIGHEST PRIORITY

While former president Trump may have made a number of missteps in foreign policy, he and his advisors saw problems in China that his predecessors either did not see or refused to acknowledge. Amid con-cerns about the massive and ongoing trade imbalances with China, the imposition of tariffs was a move in the right direction because it got China's attention. A truly bipartisan, well-thought-out strategy is needed to prevent China from surpassing the United States as the world's most dominant economy. This means drawing on the best minds on both sides of the aisle as well as from the private sector. Unfortunately, the United States often becomes distracted by events occurring in other countries—Israel, Iran, North Korea, Russia, and so on—as attention and national resources are funneled in multiple directions. America more than ever needs to focus its attention in a bipartisan way on the economic and military challenges that China poses. This means invest-ing more money, brain power, and government resources toward this objective. America can begin by delivering clear messages to China.

- First, China's unprovoked cyberattacks on America and its infrastructure have to stop—now. If not, China should expect America to retaliate in kind.
- Second, make it clear to China that the U.S. Navy will continue to keep sea lanes open around the world, including in the South China Sea and throughout Asia, in order to foster global trade.
- Third, America needs to restore some significant portion of the seven million manufacturing jobs that went to China over the last three decades. The CHIPS and Science Act of 2022, which allocated more than $50 billion to support America's semiconductor industry, is a recent example of how this is achievable.
- Fourth, America must continue to focus on out-innovating China in key technologies such as AI, quantum computing, and microprocessing.
- Fifth, as China is twice as responsible as America for global pollution, the United States should challenge China to do more to address the problems of global pollution and degradation.

CHAPTER TWENTY-THREE

WHO WILL WIN THE RACE?

The most exciting two minutes in all of sports is thoroughbred horse racing. Everyone's eyes are glued to the track as eighteen magnificent and finely trained horses explode out of the gate. The excitement is palpable as spectators who placed bets watch to see if their picks win, place, or show. The greatest risk is always rewarded with the largest purse going to the winning horse. More often than not, those that place or show are irrelevant.

This book is all about China racing to displace the United States as the world's preeminent economic and military power. The United States over the years has faced stiff competition for this top position—most notably Russia and then Japan—but China is its toughest and most determined competitor yet.

After three decades of unprecedented economic growth, Xi Jinping became China's leader in 2013 and decided it was time to put China in what he believes is its rightful place: first. Xi is doing everything in his power to make this happen, from his Belt and Road Initiative to his Made in China 2025 goals. To many observers, it certainly looks like the 21st century will belong to China. Will China win the race? If I were standing at the betting window, I would find it impossible to wager whether China will win, place, or show by the year 2049. Races can be surprising and are often unpredictable. Any problem, small or large, can affect the outcome. This book describes key MaxTrends® Xi Jinping is facing that will determine where China finishes.

But the race isn't totally about the competition now raging between the United States and China. The race here is also a contest between democracy and autocracy. Xi Jinping firmly holds the reins of power, which guarantees that any and all of his decisions will become law in China. In his autocracy, Xi doesn't face any realistic opposition or counterbalance to what he wants to achieve. But autocrats don't always get it right, and a lot of things can, and do, go wrong. Stumbling blocks, i.e., MaxTrends®, can derail an autocratic ruler's best-laid plans. Examples of misguided policies in China include the disastrous one-child policy and Xi Jinping's own failed Zero COVID-19.

Unlike China, the United States is a democracy, and democracies by their nature are often inefficient and slow to act. In a democracy, one political party's ideas are constantly challenged by the opposing party, and policies can remain in limbo for months or even years while the parties try to reach some sort of compromise. However, the strength of a true democracy lies in the inherent creativity that springs from a diverse and pluralistic society. Freedom promotes competition that fosters new and sometimes better ideas. Although often awkward, the United States as a democracy is certainly able to take steps to thwart Xi's and China's ambitious goals.

Before I end this book with a personal commentary on Hong Kong,[1] I wish to quote someone I consider to be the most influential leader of the 20th century—Winston Churchill. On November 11, 1947, after he had successfully led the United Kingdom through the depths of World War II, the people of England decided they no longer wanted him as their leader. His words ring true back then and still today:

> Many forms of Government have been tried, and will be tried, in this world of sin and woe. No one pretends that democracy is perfect or all-wise. Indeed it has been said that democracy is the worst form of government, except for all those other forms that have been tried from time to time....

China versus the United States. Autocracy versus democracy. We will have to watch and wait to see which ultimately emerges as the winner. The winner is not preordained, but I personally hope that, in the end, democracy will be victorious.

GOOD NIGHT, HONG KONG

*It was 1985 and my very first flight into Hong Kong. While I was
excited to visit a new country, my initial reaction was pure terror as
I stared out the window of the Boeing 747. I was convinced that we
were all about to die as our pilot frenziedly descended over densely
overcrowded Kowloon on our approach to Kai Tak Airport. Just seconds
before landing, I remember clearly seeing people, with their freshly
washed laundry flapping on the balconies of their high-rise apartments
right next to Kai Tak Airport, staring at our plane as it madly
descended toward the ground. As soon as the landing gear touched
down, all of us passengers were abruptly jerked forward as the pilot
savagely jammed on the brakes and brought our plane to a stop before it
either ran off the end of the runway into the harbor or crashed into the
terminal—the runway the pilot took depended on which way the wind
was blowing that day.*

That was then, and today is today. Kai Tak, once one of the world's
most dangerous airports, closed in 1998, and the Hong Kong I
remember no longer exists. The Hong Kong I came to know and love
was always part of China but separate and distinct because of its history.
How Hong Kong Island came to be such a bustling global financial
and trade center is in fact a bit of an accident. Throughout the 19th
century, the British through their trading companies did everything
in their power to ruthlessly exploit the Chinese tea market and source
other rare commodities desperately desired by the European merchant
classes. Satisfying this seemingly endless demand for Chinese goods
was a challenge, so the British trading companies began using coer-
cive methods, such as shamelessly scheming the Chinese people into

consuming opium. Sadly, the British were highly successful. By some estimates, nearly a third of the Chinese population by the mid-19th century was addicted to opium. The British and other trading companies didn't seem to care much about this abhorrent tactic; their only real concern was keeping the growing European middle class happily supplied with goods from the East.

This dark period is referred to in hushed tones by the Chinese as its "century of humiliation." Taking a stand to protect its people against the British tactics, the Chinese government struck back against Britain. In a brief but fierce confrontation, the British prevailed and humiliated the already broken Chinese and then enacted retributions. Needing a natural port to continue its exploitation of China, the British requested (demanded) a 150-year lease on a barren island that we now know as Hong Kong. The island of Hong Kong was just a short boat ride away from a peninsula off the coast of Southern China later known as Kowloon.

Despite such a demoralizing beginning, Hong Kong over time grew to become the premier trading port in Asia and particularly for China. After World War II ended, as China became a major center for multinational corporations doing business in China and throughout Asia, Hong Kong was proud of its own truly independent judicial system and took full advantage of its magnificent natural port to attract investors and traders from around the world. Hong Kong soon became flooded with British expatriates seeking to profit from this burgeoning economy. It was (and still is) quietly whispered among many native to Hong Kong that those British expatriates were "FILTH"—meaning "Failed in London, Tried Hong Kong." FILTH or not, it was due to the British presence and governance that many corporations, including banks and other financial centers, prospered in Hong Kong during the 150-year "lease."

One overall impression I consistently had of Hong Kong after visiting it many times was that it was extremely noisy. The roughly seven million Hong Kong residents were always working, always pushing, always aggressively trying to succeed. Some of that energy began to dissipate around 1997 when, according to the expiring treaty, Hong Kong reverted back to the control of the Chinese bureaucrats in Beijing. As part of the handover from Britain back to China, Sir Christopher Francis Patten, then governor of Hong Kong, attempted to negotiate a deal with Beijing. The deal was that for fifty years following the 1997 turnover, Beijing would promise that Hong Kong—while part of China—would remain a separate, democratically governed entity. While following the turnover in 1997 Beijing did remain basically "hands-off," its control did ramp up over time. One initial step was subtly discouraging use of the English language in schools and as the default language of business in Hong Kong. This was an unfortunate step, because the widespread use of the English language in Hong Kong was the primary reason so many multinational corporations and their expat executives and employees were happy living in Hong Kong and enrolling their children in schools there.

Beijing's increase in power over Hong Kong accelerated greatly after Xi Jinping came into power in 2013. In many ways, Hong Kong's electoral process, which up until then had been relatively open, became far more restricted. University students in particular were not pleased by this development and began to protest, slowly at first and over time intensifying their demand that Beijing honor its promise to allow Hong Kong to retain a democratic government. These protests, referred to as the "Umbrella Movement," began around 2014 as students and demonstrators attempted to occupy Hong Kong for seventy-nine days. They shut down its central business district in an effort to oppose the National People's Congress's plan to "prescreen" candidates in an upcoming election for chief executive of Hong Kong. This of course triggered strong reactions from Beijing that resulted in crackdowns and increased limitations on the press in Hong Kong.

Another proposed bill that led to riots in Hong Kong in 2019 stipulated extradition of Hong Kong citizens to Mainland China to be criminally tried for various levels of transgressions. In 2020, the Hong Kong government passed a law called the Law of the People's Republic of China on Safeguarding National Security in the Hong Kong Special Administrative Region. This security legislation was passed not in Hong Kong but rather by a Standing Committee of the National People's Congress. Broad and restrictive, the National Security Law targets terrorism, collusion with foreign organizations, subversion, and secession. Basically, any effort to encourage Hong Kong to secede from China either by open speech or by demonstration is considered a crime, and the law itself is administered by an office not in Hong Kong.

The riots in 2019 were not unique; there had been similar protests and mass demonstrations two decades earlier throughout Hong Kong. This time was different, though, as the new law went beyond targeting individual protesters. It also targeted internet service providers, newspaper publishers, and online hosting services. To the extent that an organization was found to be in violation of the National Security Law, the entire operation could be shut down and its employees subject to detention by Hong Kong authorities. The National Security Law was criticized by many nations around the world, and there were muted objections in Hong Kong (including by the Hong Kong Bar Association), but the threat of being arrested or detained stifled any significant objections there. Many individuals objecting to the law have been detained or otherwise prosecuted. For example, the *Apple Daily* was at one time a significant publication in Hong Kong. Because of its democratic content, its founder Jimmy Lai was arrested and imprisoned. Ultimately the assets of the *Apple Daily* were seized and the publication was shuttered.

Xi Jinping and the Chinese Communist Party, through strict enforcement of the National Security Law, have clearly succeeded in controlling public demonstrations and silencing those promoting the continued democratization of Hong Kong. Xi has decided not to honor Beijing's promise that Hong Kong could remain separate and apart from China until 2049. However, China's reputation continues to suffer from the crackdowns that in many ways call into question whether Xi's efforts were actually worthwhile. For example, Hong Kong for decades reigned as the financial center of Asia. While Beijing has constantly promoted Shanghai and other Mainland Chinese cities as global financial centers, none could match the vibrancy and accessibility of Hong Kong. Hong Kong also for decades served as the place where the renminbi (or the yuan) was freely traded in exchange for hard currencies. Now this has diminished.

Historically, excluding Japan, the preferred center for corporate headquarters in Asia has usually been in one of two places—Hong Kong or Singapore. Because of the political crackdowns in Hong Kong, many financial and other institutions have or will be faced with the decision of remaining in Hong Kong or moving their headquarters elsewhere. The bottom line is that no global business can succeed without the right people being placed in the regional headquarters. But today, expatriates who would otherwise prefer to live, work, and raise their families in Hong Kong are being discouraged from doing so. Another attraction to Hong Kong for multinational companies was its independent judiciary and international tribunal system. For years, arbitrations brought between Chinese entities and foreign companies were conducted in Hong Kong through the auspices of the highly respected Hong Kong International Arbitration Centre (HKIAC). Having an independent judiciary in Hong Kong with the ability to enforce decisions by arbitral tribunals gave multinational companies great confidence that they could reasonably resolve disputes and enforce judgments in Hong Kong. Now, a more politically structured judiciary will incentivize companies to move out of Hong Kong, and this could seriously affect the Port of Hong Kong and its status as a major trading country. Finally, as China asserts itself as not just an economic but a global leader, much of its reputation depends on its ability to keep promises in trade deals and other international forums. But no matter how persuasive, China's refusal to honor the fifty-year agreement of Hong Kong merging into China raises questions about whether China in the end will keep any of its promises. And while strict enforcement of the National Security Law appears likely to remain a significant barrier to future demonstrations, it is anyone's guess how the people in Hong Kong will ultimately react.

One final memory of Hong Kong still haunts me. I was visiting there on a business trip in June 1989 and staying in a hotel in Central, which is Hong Kong's business district. I mentioned before how Hong Kong was always a loud and boisterous place, but in my hotel room one night, I suddenly realized there was no sound. There was a total, absolute, chilling quiet. I went to my hotel balcony to see what was wrong, and there, on the streets below, were thousands upon thousands of Hong Kong citizens holding candles and walking silently. No words, no sounds, simply an eerie silence. That was the night of Tiananmen Square, when democratic protests were violently and forcibly ended by the People's Liberation Army. That night nearly thirty-five years ago was permeated by the quiet desperation of the people of Hong Kong passionately defending their democratic system and way of life.

THE IMPACT OF CFIUS AND FIRRMA ON POTENTIAL FOREIGN INVESTMENTS IN AMERICA

Because America remains a preferred destination for foreign direct investment (FDI), investors from around the world are constantly seeking opportunities within the large U.S. economy. Some see investing in the United States as a way to circumvent tariffs and various imposed trade barriers, while others are interested in acquiring valuable technologies that can provide competitive advantages. Legal barriers are now more stringent for foreign entities interested in investing in America and its technologies than in the past. It became more challenging when the Foreign Investment Risk Review Modernization Act of 2018 (FIRRMA) was signed into law on August 13, 2018. FIRRMA was intended to update and strengthen the powers of the Committee on Foreign Investment in the United States (CFIUS), which plays a key role in regulating FDI. In the end, FIRRMA has made the process and time required to finalize foreign investments in the U.S. more challenging than in the past.

Prior to the passage of FIRRMA, three key laws and sets of regulations primarily governed foreign investments targeting the United States. First, the Exon-Florio Act of 1988 (Exon-Florio) was ratified in the mid-1980s in direct response to growing fears within the U.S. Congress about the aggressive and widespread acquisitions of significant American businesses and real estate properties by Japanese multinationals. In its simplest terms, Exon-Florio gives the president power to halt a proposed purchase or reverse a completed transaction between an American entity and a foreign investor if (1) credible evidence exists that the transaction would negatively impact U.S. national security, and (2) there are no steps the president is willing to approve to minimize those effects. As a result of Exon-Florio, foreign investors are best advised to analyze well in advance the potential national security implications of any possible project in the U.S. before making a public announcement and proceeding.

EXON-FLORIO AND FIRRMA

Exon-Florio was significantly upgraded following the September 11, 2001, terrorist attacks on New York City and Washington, DC. The new law, the Foreign Investment and National Security Act (FINSA), imposed more comprehensive scrutiny on all kinds of investments in the United States. Under FINSA, FDI transactions involving "critical infrastructure" in the U.S. received a more rigorous governmental review. For example, the 2006 purchase by Dubai Ports World (DP World) of the British-owned Peninsular and Oriental Steam Navigation Company gave DP World control over a number of key ports in the U.S., including Philadelphia, Miami, New Orleans, New York, Newark, and Baltimore. The task for government regulators is to decide whether permitting foreign companies control of American ports poses such a national security risk that the U.S. government should intercede to block the deal. FINSA obligates the U.S. government's executive branch to periodically report to Congress if and how national security interests may be harmed by FDI transactions. When a possible transaction involves a legal entity controlled or owned by a foreign government, FINSA mandates a formal examination of the proposed deal. This involves (1) a foreign entity that is (2) possibly acquiring control of an American business that (3) possesses products, services, or intellectual property that are (4) important to U.S. national security or critical to U.S. infrastructure. The definition of a foreign entity is "any foreign national, foreign government, foreign entity, or any other entity over which control is exercised or exercisable by a foreign national, foreign government, or foreign entity." It is important to remember that CFIUS only reviews transactions involving existing businesses. It does not apply to "Greenfield" investments where a foreign party has decided to start a business from the ground up. Definitions of "national security" and "critical infrastructure," though, are not sufficiently clear and so are extremely broad and subject to regular updates and changes.

TWO CFIUS OPTIONS

When considering an investment in the United States and weighing whether a CFIUS review will be part of the process, foreign investors need to choose between two options. The first option involves voluntarily giving advance notice to CFIUS. Unless advance notice is mandated, a foreign investor can elect to submit to CFIUS in advance the details of its intention to make a particular investment in the United States. The foreign investor in its application voluntarily discloses to CFIUS the nature, purpose, scope, and expected closing date of the transaction. The assets to be acquired are listed and described along with information about the investor itself, including a description of its business activities and any ties it may have to foreign governments or agencies.

The second option is for a foreign investor to not give any notice to CFIUS of a potential deal. If a foreign government is not directly involved, a foreign investor (with some exceptions under FIRRMA) may elect to proceed without advising CFIUS in advance. However, there can be consequences if a potential investor chooses this option. The major risk is that if CFIUS later reviews and rejects the deal after it is complete, then the U.S. government can order the deal reversed.

There is no time limitation on CFIUS's ability to look back and review a closed transaction, and this constitutes a serious commercial risk for any company.

CFIUS REVIEW PERIOD

Before a transaction closes, there is a specific timeframe (in theory) within which CFIUS must act. The majority of transactions for which CFIUS is given advance notice for review are supposed to be cleared within forty-five days. However, that is not a realistic guideline for investors because most reviews go beyond the forty-five-day notice period. Of 286 applications that were filed in 2022, 162 went on for further examination during the investigation period. It is not unusual for examinations to take several months or more. As a result, it is common for about 30 percent of the filed applications to be withdrawn.

If the proposed transaction clears, it has "safe harbor" protection, meaning the CFIUS decision is final and cannot be reversed (unless, of course, the investor misrepresented information or acted fraudulently). Once a proposed FDI project is sent to the president, the president has fifteen days to review the transaction and reach a final decision. Presidential decisions are not subject to judicial review.

MITIGATION AGREEMENTS

If CFIUS determines that a proposed FDI transaction will result in foreign ownership or control of an American business that will have negative national security implications, the foreign investor can request the opportunity to negotiate with the U.S. government to complete the transaction to the mutual satisfaction of both parties. These mitigation agreements are becoming more common. If successful, CFIUS and the parties execute a mitigation agreement outlining the changes necessary to satisfy any concerns regarding national security. CFIUS frequently requires mitigation agreements in the form of board resolutions, security control agreements, special security agreements, proxy agreements, and/or voting trust agreements. Once a mitigation agreement is approved and the transaction is completed, CFIUS has the authority to continue monitoring ongoing compliance with the agreement.

THE FOREIGN INVESTMENT RISK REVIEW MODERNIZATION ACT OF 2018

On August 13, 2018, the Foreign Investment Risk Review Modernization Act of 2018 was signed into law. FIRRMA significantly expands what role CFIUS will play when reviewing foreign investments in the United States. A primary goal of this law is to prevent the theft of trade secrets and intellectual property of American companies as well as keep foreign companies from investing in or purchasing assets near U.S. military bases. FIRRMA strengthens and expands the CFIUS review process and makes it more difficult for foreign companies to successfully invest in the United States if national security interests are at risk.

FIRRMA made some substantial changes to CFIUS review procedures. While the original jurisdiction of CFIUS did not change, parties face a more challenging and complex analysis when deciding whether to file for clearance under FIRRMA regulations. The underlying issue is whether a CFIUS filing is "mandatory." Transactions are no longer limited to those that result in the "foreign control" of a business. CFIUS can look at transactions proposing any level of foreign control by the investor.

There are two rationales for asserting CFIUS jurisdiction. The first is "defined real estate transactions" and the second is "TID[1] U.S. Businesses," which are defined as businesses that are involved in critical technologies, critical infrastructure, and/or sensitive personal data.

CFIUS is authorized to review certain investments that are viewed as "noncontrolling" but not fully passive in nature. The U.S. government is concerned when a noncontrolling investment results in a foreign person having (1) membership rights or observer rights on a TID U.S. business board of directors; (2) any involvement in decision-making in a TID U.S. business (other than simply voting shares); or (3) access to substantive nonpublic proprietary information of a TID U.S. business.

FIRRMA regulations define what is necessary to be considered as a TID U.S. business. "Critical technologies" include items on the Commerce Control List (CCL), software, defense materials, and emerging technology. "Critical infrastructure" industries include oil and gas, telecoms, water, finance, defense industries, ports, and power. Companies handling sensitive personal data are also covered, including individual personal data, data collection, and genetic information. Because of FIRRMA, some real estate transactions are subject to CFIUS review and approval. Examples include real estate located near military bases, missile fields, and/or maritime ports and airports. There are exceptions so that many types of real estate purchases are not subject to CFIUS review and approval.

The U.S. government becomes concerned when foreign governments are involved in TID U.S. businesses. This is an area where CFIUS requires a filing at least thirty days prior to a controlled transaction. Investment funds are another area where a careful review of FIRRMA regulations is required. Some types of investments are covered by both CFIUS and FIRRMA.

In 2023, the Biden Administration issued Executive Orders promising that CFIUS will no longer focus primarily on inbound foreign investments. In the future, CFIUS and its authority will expand to include the review of certain types of outbound transactions that may harm U.S. national security interests. This will impact U.S. investment entities doing business internationally and will be interesting to follow into 2024 and beyond.

In short, the scope of CFIUS reviews continuously broadens, and the numbers of filings that require additional investigation continue to grow. The process promises to become ever more complex.

EIGHT EXAMPLES OF GLOBAL FDI REGULATIONS

How China and the United States review and regulate inbound foreign direct investment continues to expand in numbers and scope. However, the U.S. and China are not alone. What follows are policies regarding FDI adopted by the United Kingdom, Germany, France, Italy, Spain, the Netherlands, Japan, and Canada. Though there are many similarities among these policies, each country has some of its own unique laws.

UNITED KINGDOM. The United Kingdom has taken a very aggressive stance much like the United States, and in many ways tracks CFIUS regulations and the U.S. Foreign Investment Risk Review Modernization Act of 2018. The British law known as the National Security and Investment Act (NSI Act) came into effect in 2022. Providing for mandatory filings, over one thousand transactions per year are reviewed. Any company doing business with or supplying services or goods into the United Kingdom may find themselves under the purview of the NSI Act. This would include the acquisition of assets such as intellectual property and, in some cases, real estate. The UK's previous act, the Enterprise Act of 2002, only provided a limited review of investments, particularly as they applied to bribe casting. However, much like in the United States, the NSI Act is triggered when national security interests are affected. Under the law, the UK secretary of state for business, energy, and industrial strategy has the power to review transactions (even after they are closed) if the secretary believes the transaction may have adversely affected national security interests in the UK. Even for transactions that do not presently require manda-tory review, the UK has the power to review the transaction for up to five years afterward. As in the United States, the NSI Act considers specific sectors of the economy that are considered to be sensitive, such as computing hardware, critical supplies, communications, data infrastructure, and energy. Since the NSI Act has recently become law, its effectiveness is yet to be evaluated. But the point is that, like CFIUS, it will stand as a barrier to foreign direct investment that in any way could impact security interests.

GERMANY. Germany's Federal Ministry of Economics (BMWi) has set its threshold at 25 percent voting rights or assets for general transactions. In its protected sectors—which include defense, criti-cal infrastructures, telecommunications, healthcare, and media—the threshold is 10 percent. The BMWi also requires that the parties involved in the transaction notify the ministry and provide proper documenta-tion of their intentions and involvement with other governments prior to approval of the transaction in protected sectors. The review process can take anywhere between two and seven months. If it is uncertain whether the transaction in an unprotected sector may pose a risk to national security, the investor may apply for a certificate of nonobjec-tion, which, if approved, means the government has approved the transaction. If not notified, the BMWi reserves the right to review the transaction for up to five years following its completion.

FRANCE. France's Ministry of Economy (MOE) requires prior authorization for investments for: (1) the acquisition of control of a French entity; (2) the acquisition in whole or otherwise of a French business; and (3) the crossing, directly or indirectly, alone or in con-cert with third parties, of the threshold of 25 percent voting rights in a French entity. When the threshold is met, the MOE is required to be notified. The MOE has set its threshold at 25 percent voting rights or purchase of whole or part of a business line or acquisition of controlling interest. However, worth noting is that until December 31, 2020, the threshold was set at 10 percent to protect French businesses during the COVID-19 pandemic. France's protected sectors include defense, dual-use technologies, surveillance, gambling, critical infrastructures, and research and development.

ITALY. For entities that do not reside, own a registered or administrative office, or have a center of interests in the European Union, the threshold for Italy is set at 10 percent voting rights or investment value representing 10 percent of the domestic company's corporate capital. With regard to entities affiliated with the European Union, the threshold is set at acquisition of a controlling interest in the domestic company. Italy's protected sectors include defense, dual-use technologies, critical infrastructure supplies and technologies, agriculture, media, and finances. The review process can take anywhere between forty-five and sixty business days.

SPAIN. As a response to COVID-19 and EU regulations, Spain has set its investment threshold at 10 percent of capital share or acquisition of control over a Spanish company in nondefense sectors. In defense sectors, all acquisitions have to be filed with the Spanish government. Spain's protected sectors include defense, critical infrastructures, technologies and supplies, sensitive data, and media. When the investment is made in protected sectors, the government must be notified. The review process takes six months.

THE NETHERLANDS. Dutch law tends to be more liberal in its approach. It does not provide general restrictions or a framework for the FDI screening process except in specific sectors that are considered vital in either the perspective of public interest or security. However, its protected sectors include defense, energy, telecommunications, drinking water, nuclear energy, mining, and underground gas storage.

JAPAN. Japan's Ministry of Finance (MOF) has lowered its threshold from 10 to 1 percent for pretransaction approval for acquisition by foreign investors of shares in Japanese-listed companies in designated sectors. As such, investors must file with the MOF if they plan to buy more than a 1 percent stake in the designated firms. If a foreign investor already has at least 1 percent of the shares, prior notification for pretransaction approval is required for any additional purchases of shares in the company. The protected sectors include weapons, aircraft, nuclear facilities, space, dual-use technologies, cybersecurity, electricity, gas, telecommunications, water supply, rail, and oil. The review process is thirty days (but can be longer).

CANADA. Canada uses a two-factor test for determining if a pretransaction notification is necessary. The factors considered are "size of the parties" and "size of the transaction." Under the size-of-the-parties approach, the parties in conjunction with their affiliates must have assets in Canada or annual gross revenue from sales in, from, or into Canada that exceed C$400 million. Under the size-of-the-transaction approach, the value of the Canadian assets or the gross revenue from sales created by those assets in or from Canada of the target operating business must be greater than C$96 million. The transaction-size component can be adjusted each year to account for inflation. The review process takes forty-five days. Canada's protected sectors are public health and critical goods and services.

THE DIFFERENT FACES
OF CORRUPTION

Defining corruption is about as hard as defining love. What is love? There are many different kinds: parental love, romantic love, platonic love, love of one's country, love of life, and so on. In the same way, trying to tie all types of corruption into one simple bundle can be impossible. Dictionaries define "corruption" as a form of dishonesty, outright bribery, or lack of integrity. The term is commonly used when referring to the improper conduct of public officials selling "favors" for money or other personal benefits. However, any simple definition of corruption is misleading. Corruption is exceptionally difficult to define when it applies to China because the laws in China are opaque. Corruption in China often is referred to as "violations of law and party discipline." The phrase has its genesis with the Chinese Communist Party, which dispenses discipline that comes from its own set of rules and regulations.

One global nongovernmental agency, Transparency International (TI), exists to track and quantify the quality and degree of corruption in countries around the world. Based in Berlin, TI for the last quarter century has published its annual *Corruption Perceptions Index* (the "TI Index"). The TI Index ranks 180 countries according to their level of corruption based on the polled opinions of "knowledgeable individuals." The two countries ranked highest on the TI Index—meaning they are the least corrupt—are New Zealand and Denmark. Economically advanced countries tend to rank higher on the list, and developing countries tend to rank lower. Take India, which is ranked eighty-sixth on the TI Index, while Brazil lands even lower. These TI rankings, though, can be misleading. Singaporean-born academic Yuen Ang is an associate professor and Chinese scholar at the University of Michigan. Professor Ang, finding the TI ranking system too simplistic, created a method assigning corruption into one of four basic types: petty theft, grand theft, speed money, and access money. *Petty theft* basically involves stealing or extortion among lower-level officials. *Grand theft* covers more serious activities such as embezzlement or misappropriation of funds. Examples of *speed money* include bribes that bureaucrats might receive in order to hasten decisions or allow an individual or entity to jump ahead of someone else. The fourth type of corruption according to Professor Ang, *access money*, is the interaction between businesspeople and influential government officials who can "make things happen." This is when the concept of *guanxi* in China is most apparent. In other words, private connections between powerful people can lead to outcomes that might not otherwise be permitted.[1]

Americans should be careful about being too critical of what they perceive as corruption in China, because while America operates differently than China, it has its own forms of corruption. It is common (and legal) for wealthy U.S. corporations, individuals, and organizations to aggressively influence public policy by lobbying, which in America is not considered to be corruption or even inappropriate.

IS CHINA FOLLOWING THE JAPAN MODEL?

W hile a student at the University of Virginia, I developed a life-long fascination with two countries: Japan and China. I have been fortunate throughout my career to have visited both countries more times than I can actually count (my assistant actually tried once and gave up). After nearly four decades and more than one hundred trips to Japan in particular, I believe that the history of Japan over the last three centuries is helpful in predicting the future direction of China. One example is China's decade-long drive under Xi Jinping to massively expand China's military capabilities, which in some ways parallels periods of transformation throughout Japan's history.

Beginning around the year 1650, Japan voluntarily withdrew from the rest of the world, cutting itself off from most foreign influences and trade (except for two ports that were carefully monitored by the powerful Shoguns). Japan's period of self-imposed isolation lasted over two hundred years, ending abruptly when U.S. Naval Commodore Matthew Calbraith Perry arrived unannounced in Japan in 1853. Admiral Perry docked in Tokyo Bay at Yokosuka with orders to deliver a formal written message from U.S. president Millard Fillmore to the Japanese emperor. The message contained in President Fillmore's letter was simple but firm—Japan was to open up diplomatic relations and its ports to American vessels and trade. After initially refusing to meet with Admiral Perry, the Japanese eventually delivered the message from President Fillmore to the emperor. His mission fulfilled,

Admiral Perry sailed back to America, but he returned to Japan early in 1854. This time, Perry was accompanied by his "black ships"—which were armed to the teeth—as he sought a formal response from Japan's emperor. After several weeks of negotiations, the Japanese ultimately conceded. Slowly at first, trade began to flow between Japan and the United States as diplomatic relations were established. This somewhat uneasy partnership was interrupted by the outbreak of the U.S. Civil War in 1861. During that critical junction in American history, the majority of U.S. Navy vessels were withdrawn from the Pacific Ocean and reassigned to fight the Confederacy until its defeat in 1865.

Through it all, the Japanese remained highly resentful of Admiral Perry's unwelcome arrival on their shores and President Fillmore's demand to engage in foreign trade. Forced against its will to open its borders, Japan reversed course and for the next eighty years adopted an aggressive military posture. Japan accomplished this by rapidly expanding its naval capabilities, something that China is pursuing today.

Then, during the 1930s, Japanese militarists invaded Manchuria and later brutally attacked China in Shanghai and Nanjing. At that point, Japan made a terrible strategic decision for which it paid a high price. Because the British in the 1930s were embargoing Japan from oil and rubber sourced in Southeast Asia, Japanese military commanders decided to attack both Singapore and Pearl Harbor at the same time, the intent being to force the British out of Southeast Asia and U.S. Navy vessels out of the Pacific. This again looks a lot like China's dominance in the South China Sea. Obviously, Japan's plan failed, and its unprovoked attack on Pearl Harbor was exactly the impetus President Franklin D. Roosevelt needed in order to get a protectionist-oriented America to declare war against Japan and join World War II. The attack on Pearl Harbor forced America to conduct a war on two fronts and, as a result, massive amounts of resources went into ramping up the U.S. Navy in the Pacific and Atlantic theaters. Thus, at the end of World War II, America emerged with the world's only blue-water navy, which over the next forty years, except for occasional skirmishes with the Soviets, went essentially unchallenged.

In the same way Japan was forced by external sources to become a global player in 1854, China is following a similar path. Between the death of Mao Zedong in 1976 and the entry of Xi Jinping onto the world stage in 2012, China remained essentially inward-looking except when it came to trade. China did everything it could for thirty years to attract foreign direct investment, and it succeeded. Also, like Japan in the 1930s, China today is aiming to secure its own blue-water presence throughout the Pacific. Now that China is the second largest economy in the world, Xi Jinping has decided that China's military, instead of being primarily defensive, should evolve into a force that is increasingly offensive in nature. China's aggressive military maneuvers focusing on Taiwan and its naval bases located throughout the South China Sea signal China's intention to establish itself as the dominant force throughout the Pacific region. I have no crystal ball, but it is worth remembering how Japan acted almost a century ago and how its decisions changed the world.

A LAYMAN'S GUIDE TO UNDERSTANDING INTELLECTUAL PROPERTY PROTECTION

Note: Some of the information contained in this appendix comes from The Trade Secrets Handbook *(Prentice-Hall, Englewood Cliffs, NJ, 1985). I am the author of that book. As both an author and a practicing lawyer, I highly value how intellectual property laws can effectively protect technologies, unique ideas, and writings, and those who create them.*

Intellectual property (IP) laws are the various legal methods available to protect innovative ideas and confidential information, forms of expressing ideas (such as writing or music), and unique names and symbols. There are four basic ways to protect intellectual property: (1) patents; (2) copyrights; (3) trademarks/service marks; and (4) trade secrets.

PATENTS. The Constitution of the United States (Article I, Section 8) provides that inventors are granted certain legal protections for their creations. For example, the creator of an invention can apply for a patent that, if granted, gives the patent owner the sole right to produce, use, and/or sell the protected invention for a set period of time. The philosophy behind patent protection is that, in exchange for the inventor providing a full and complete disclosure of their invention and later allowing this information to be used by the general public, the inventor is granted a limited monopoly over the invention during the life of the patent (generally fifteen years for a design patent and twenty years for a utility patent).

America has a long and proud history of protecting its patent owners and their inventions during the life of the patents. Highly prized during the Industrial Revolution of the 19th and early 20th centuries, patents in the United States constituted a crucial strategic element in the development and rise of many large corporations that continue to play an important role in the American economy. Traditionally, patents were considered valuable because the patented products or formulations had an expected long commercial life extending to well after the patent protections had expired.

When competing in a global economy, patent protection granted in one country does not guarantee that same coverage will be honored by other countries. If a patented item is to be used or sold internationally, separate patent filings are necessary in those countries where markets are being considered for the patented technologies. Simply put, if a patent is filed for and granted in the United States, and the owner subsequently fails to obtain similar patent protection in targeted foreign markets, foreign competitors are legally free to produce similar products.[1] While it seems like an obvious choice to apply for patent protection in countries where the technology may be used and sold, the significant filing costs and lengthy, complex disclosures required in order to obtain patent protection in multiple jurisdictions are often disincentives. Patents may also require the payment of yearly maintenance fees, which can be expensive.

COPYRIGHTS. A copyright (©) is another right granted under the U.S. Constitution; however, the protections provided by a copyright are less broad than those granted by a patent. Entirely distinct and different from a patent, a copyright is available to authors of literary, dramatic, musical, artistic, and other kinds of intellectual works. A copyright can protect the physical manifestation of a particular document or work of art and provides authors with the exclusive right to publish, print, distribute, copy, or perform their works. The act of copyrighting applies not to just works of art, but also to photographs, pictorial illustrations, product labels, business books, technical manuals, advertising and sales literature, and most business-related information that is in tangible form.

It is important to stress that a copyright does not prevent someone else from independently working toward the same result. While this book is copyrighted and may not be directly reproduced without the copyright holder's (my) permission, anyone is free to write on the topic of China as long as the ideas are their own and not a mirror image of this particular book. That is the major difference between patenting and obtaining a copyright. While a copyright certainly provides some legal protection for authors, for most businesses the value of the protection available under a copyright is probably not helpful if a business seeks to keep corporate information away from competitors. Copyrighting demands disclosure, and that is the exact opposite of what some businesses desire.

TRADEMARKS. Different from either a patent or a copyright, a trademark (™) or "service mark" is available to an individual or company desiring to protect a logo, word, or phrase that is used to identify unique goods or services or ideas. For example, I have applied for and received trademark protection for the words "MaxTrend" and "MaxTrends." The purpose of a trademark is to protect individuals or businesses from having others adopt a similar mark for another product that would be confusingly similar. While "common law trademarks" can exist under individual state laws, the most desirable trademarks are those that are officially registered with the U.S. Patent and Trademark Office. Those trademarks receive far more significant protection in federal courts than those that are not registered. In 1946, the U.S. Congress passed the Lanham Act (15 U.S.C. §§1051-1127), which granted the U.S. Patent and Trademark Office the authority to oversee and regulate federal trademark registrations. As with other types of intellectual property, the applicant should file for protection in all individual countries (or a collective registration such as the European Union) where the trademark will be used in order to guarantee protection outside the United States.

TRADE SECRETS. It is often the case that information is either not eligible for protection as a patent, copyright, or trademark, or that an individual or company decides not to use those forms of intellectual property protection. Those are cases where protection can fall under the form of trade secrets. While a precise definition is elusive, there are three basic elements that constitute a trade secret: *novelty, value,* and *secrecy.* When trying to decide whether an idea or item of information should be viewed and thus protected as a trade secret, applying these three criteria is helpful in making that determination. "Novelty" means that the information, document, or formulation cannot be commonplace or readily available to anybody outside of the company. Next, "value" means that the information is vital to a company's operations and would also be of benefit to a company's competitors if it were to be made known. Finally, a trade secret must, as the name implies, be kept "secret," and appropriate steps must be taken to ensure that the information does not become available to the public. If that happens, its trade-secret status is lost. The scope of what can be protected as a trade secret is very broad. Examples can include:

- Unpatented products.
- Individual formulations, such as the chemical makeup of cleaning products or ingredients in cosmetics.
- Industrial processes: not necessarily specific pieces of equipment but rather *how* they are used.

- A piece of machinery purchased in the ordinary course of business is not a trade secret, but modifying that machine in a unique manner might be.
- Research and development documentation of a company's activities, including blueprints, drawings, computer-generated data, and test results.
- Corporate correspondence that in some way would reveal operations or activities to a competitor.
- Financial, accounting, and customer information.
- Long-term corporate planning or internal marketing strategies whose confidentiality an individual works to maintain.

Often the term "know-how" is used during a discussion of trade secrets. Sort of a distant cousin of trade secrets, know-how is often not available like other forms of intellectual property. Applying the three criteria of novelty, value, and secrecy helps in drawing the line between what is know-how and what is a trade secret. While know-how may have genuine value to a corporation, it in itself may not be novel or unique. Know-how is best described as information developed or accumulated by a business that is helpful in the operation of the business. Know-how is not as critically important to business activity as are trade secrets. For this reason, employees are normally not as strictly regulated in how they handle know-how as they would be if working with their employer's trade secrets.

As an example, assume a company has a continuous casting operation for high-quality steel production. A specific machine used in the assembly line can be viewed as a trade secret if the design of the machine is proprietary. The exact mixture of materials to form the proper steel slurry could also be a trade secret. However, the floor layout for the equipment would more likely be know-how, as would the timing of when certain materials are introduced into the process.

An hourly employee who worked with the continuous casting operation for years and developed a keen understanding of the best ways to maximize productivity would possess valuable know-how. A close relationship exists between know-how and trade secrets, and there is a fine line between the two, so that a company must apply the same techniques to shield both valuable trade secrets and internal know-how from outsiders.

CHINA VERSUS THE UNITED STATES: A STUDY IN OPPOSITES

It is difficult to overstate how fundamentally different the United States and China are. This is what makes their intense economic (and at times military) competition and future relationship so difficult to predict. One significant difference is that China's population is four times larger than that of the United States. Yet, China's GDP still trails the United States (though the gap is narrowing). The table below highlights some of the differences between the two countries.

China versus the U.S.	
China[1]	**United States**
Population: 1.41 billion	Population: 335 million
2022 est. GDP: $17.9 trillion	2022 est. GDP: $25.4 trillion
Range of annual growth: 3% to 8%	Range of annual growth: 2% to 4%
Ethnicity: 91% of the population is Han Chinese	Ethnicity: Diverse
Urban population: 61.4% Rural population: 38.6%	Urban population: 82.7% Rural population: 17.3%
Middle class: 350 million to 400 million people	Middle class: Depending on the survey, between 25% and 60% of U.S. households
Primary agricultural industries: Maize, rice, vegetables, wheat, sugar cane, potatoes, cucumbers, tomatoes, watermelons, sweet potatoes	Primary agricultural industries: Maize, milk, soybeans, wheat, sugar cane, sugar beets, poultry, potatoes, cotton, pork, milk

China versus the U.S.	
China[1]	United States
Primary industries: Mining and ore processing, iron, steel, aluminum, coal, machine building, armaments, textiles/apparel, petroleum, cement, chemicals, fertilizer, consumer products, food processing, transportation equipment/automobiles, railcars/locomotives, ships, aircraft, telecommunications equipment, commercial space launch vehicles, satellites	Primary industries: High-technology innovation, petroleum, steel, motor vehicles, aerospace, telecommunications, chemicals, electronics, food processing, consumer goods, lumber, mining
Government: Autocracy controlled by the Chinese Communist Party	Government: Democracy

HOW CHINA BECAME A WORLD POWER

Considering its extraordinary record of economic growth and development, it is hard to imagine that China was until relatively recently one of the poorest countries in the world. During the 1960s, China suffered widespread starvation, particularly in its rural areas, resulting in millions of deaths. The policies promoted by Mao Zedong contributed to China's desperate state. Things began to change after the economic and political relationship between China and the United States was jumpstarted by former president Richard Nixon. Nixon was a staunch anti-Communist Republican, but in 1972 he made a bold and unexpected move with his historic visit to China as an American president. Nixon signaled an interest in developing better commercial relationships between American and Chinese companies for the first time. However, few substantive business ventures were actually consummated over the next six years since foreign direct investment into China was prohibited under Chinese laws. Mao died in 1976, but even into the late 1970s, China's role in the global marketplace (excluding Hong Kong and Taiwan) remained extremely limited, as less than 10 percent of China's national income involved foreign trade. China desperately needed foreign investment to jumpstart its economy.

CHINA AFTER MAO

Significant shifts began to occur after the death of Mao Zedong in 1976. In 1978, China announced its first "open door" policy, which was aimed at attracting much-needed foreign capital and technologies, particularly from the United States and Europe. This radical new policy for the Chinese was a brilliant strategic move made possible by China's new leader, Deng Xiaoping. Deng faced down China's conservative leadership and forced the reversal of traditional opposition to foreign trade because he realized foreign investment and technology were the only ways that a modernized, industrial China could evolve. Over the next three decades, China continuously updated its laws and implemented governmental regulations that specifically targeted and encouraged foreign investment. It was slow at first. From 1979 to 1986, only 7,500 foreign investment contracts and memorandums of understanding were signed in China, with an estimated value of US$19.1 billion. However, after 1986, the number of inbound foreign investments increased twentyfold, transforming China from an underdeveloped country into the world's second largest economy.

The death of Deng Xiaoping in February 1997 marked yet another transition for China, as a new and younger generation of leadership took charge. Deng's handpicked successor, Jiang Zemin, did not attempt to derail the revolutionary initiatives Deng had championed. Instead, Jiang promised to accelerate the economic policies Deng had launched. This held true until 2002, when China's top leadership again changed. Around September 2004, after a two-year transition period, Jiang Zemin formally ceded all of his official leadership positions to his successor, Hu Jintao. Continuing forward with the initiatives begun by Deng and Jiang, Hu aggressively encouraged foreign direct investment in China and redirected the capital generated by export sales to further underwrite China's infrastructure.

CHINA'S ECONOMY

Annual economic growth rates in China over the last three and a half decades have been historic and unprecedented. While more modest in 2001 and 2002, China's growth returned to torrid levels from 2003 to 2008, sometimes at over 10 percent per year. In October 2008, China was hit by the widespread Asian Economic Crisis, but, surprisingly, China's economy began to grow once again in 2009 and rebounded to 10.3 percent in 2010. China expanded 9.2 percent in 2011, slightly less in 2012. This was the time when Xi Jinping ascended to China's top leadership position.

China's economy leveled out to 6 to 7 percent growth per year over the next half decade (though it is important to note that 6 to 7 percent annual growth is still one of the highest growth rates anywhere). But since 2017, China's growth has significantly fallen. In 2022, China's economy grew at only 3 percent. One reason (other than COVID-19) was that factory output has slowed as the cost of Chinese labor has risen. This led to some factories relocating from China to Vietnam, Bangladesh, Malaysia, India, and elsewhere in Southeast Asia where labor costs were significantly lower.

For decades, China's production capacity targeted sales of manufactured goods into export markets, and China deliberately developed its infrastructure and structured its supply chain to meet these demands. A now evident trend is China's growing domestic consumer market, which means China is no longer exclusively focusing on manufacturing goods for export. Increasing percentages of what is produced in China now go toward satisfying the demands of Chinese consumers, most of whom are part of China's middle class. With about 1.41 billion potential domestic consumers in China, this trend will continue.

CHINA AND THE SUPPLY CHAIN

China's commercial base is made up of state-owned enterprises and private companies. The SOEs, which represent between 50 and 60 percent of the overall Chinese economy, are directly controlled by and financed through China's central government. This relationship gives SOEs access to vast financial resources in major industries such as chemicals, steel, and petroleum (though it is worth noting that SOEs are traditionally viewed as inefficient). The remaining companies in China are private but, as described throughout this book, highly pressured by the Chinese government through its direct and indirect influence over their operations.

GLOSSARY

3D PRINTING (ALSO KNOWN AS 3D MANUFACTURING OR ADDITIVE MANUFACTURING) A technology that captures a three-dimensional image in a digital or CAD format and then reproduces an exact replica on a machine aptly named a 3D printer. The 3D printer uses materials in a liquid, powder, or metallic form and fuses the materials into exceptionally thin layers.

AI (ARTIFICIAL INTELLIGENCE) In its most basic form, AI refers to how a machine learns so that the machine is able to replicate human thinking, enabling it to solve problems or follow directions independently.

ARAB LEAGUE Also known as the "League of Arab States," the Arab League was formed in 1945 and is a regional organization of countries located in Northern, Western, and Eastern Africa and in Western Asia.

ASEAN (ASSOCIATION OF SOUTHEAST ASIAN NATIONS) Formed in 1967, ASEAN is currently made up of ten member states (Brunei, Cambodia, Indonesia, Laos, Malaysia, Myanmar, the Philippines, Singapore, Thailand, and Vietnam). Its goal is to promote political, educational, and social integration among its members.

BELT AND ROAD INITIATIVE This massive initiative was undertaken by the Chinese government in order to invest in infrastructure and other development projects. The Belt and Road Initiative was begun in 2013, and through it China hopes to ultimately invest in more than 145 countries and international organizations.

BIS (Bureau of Industry Security) Part of the U.S. government, the BIS operates to protect national security by overseeing a complex export control and treaty compliance system.

Blue-water strategy (blue-water navy) "Blue water" is the term used to describe maritime capabilities, specifically the ability of a nation's navy to operate globally at long-range distances in deepwater oceans, often simultaneously in different locales. It is a way to project power away from the navy's home base and usually involves aircraft carriers. Currently the U.S. Navy is the only fully capable and resourced blue-water navy in the world.

Brexit An abbreviated term for "British Exit," Brexit refers to the withdrawal of the United Kingdom from the European Union, which became effective on January 31, 2020.

CAN (Andean Community) A trade bloc composed of Peru, Ecuador, Colombia, and Bolivia. Located in Lima, Peru, CAN has five other countries that are associate members, and Spain, Mexico, and Panama act as observers.

CCP (Chinese Communist Party) The sole political power bloc exercising control over 1.41 billion Chinese people. The CCP has approximately 98 million official members.

Central Military Commission Xi Jinping is the chair of the Central Military Commission, which gives him ultimate control over China's military.

CFIUS (Committee on Foreign Investment in the United States) An interagency task force that reviews proposed inbound investments or acquisitions in order to evaluate whether such projects could affect U.S. national security interests.

CHIPS AND SCIENCE ACT OF 2022 A law that authorized $50 billion to strengthen semiconductor and ICT supply chains in the United States and to promote domestic manufacturing capabilities.

CIRCIA (CYBER INCIDENT REPORTING FOR CRITICAL INFRASTRUCTURE ACT OF 2022) Signed into law in March 2022, CIRCIA promotes reporting of cyber incidents and anomalous cyber activity to the U.S. government.

CISA (U.S. CYBERSECURITY AND INFRASTRUCTURE AGENCY) Responsible for protecting cybersecurity and infrastructure throughout the U.S. government; falls under the direction of the Department of Homeland Security.

COMESA (COMMON MARKET FOR EASTERN AND SOUTHERN AFRICA) COMESA was established in 1994 and is composed of 21 member states.

COMMONWEALTH OF NATIONS An international organization composed of fifty-six member countries, most of which are former territories of the British Empire.

COUNTRY GARDEN One of the largest of the Chinese private property developers that faced serious financial problems in 2023 and 2024 due to the decline of China's real property sector.

CPTPP (COMPREHENSIVE AND PROGRESSIVE AGREEMENT FOR THE TRANS-PACIFIC PARTNERSHIP) A free trade agreement between Canada and ten countries located in the Asia-Pacific region.

CULTURAL REVOLUTION (1966–1976) A policy imposed by Mao Zedong and enforced by his Red Guards intended to purge China of any individual in the government, academia, or industry who did not favor Mao's policies.

DARPA (DEFENSE ADVANCED RESEARCH PROJECTS AGENCY) Under the U.S. Department of Defense, DARPA is a research and development agency that promotes new technologies with primarily military potential.

DEBT-TO-GDP RATIO This is an important economic measurement of the ratio between a country's government debt and its gross domestic product. The lower the ratio, the more attractive a country is to investors.

DEGLOBALIZATION A trend in which nations reject or otherwise reduce their reliance on global organizations or on cooperation and interdependence with other countries.

DENG XIAOPING The founder of modern China; its leader from 1978 to 1989; responsible for opening up China by implementing a series of market and economic reforms.

DLA (DEFENSE LOGISTICS AGENCY) An important part of the U.S. Department of Defense. Located in Fort Belvoir, Virginia, the DLA, among other functions, directly interfaces with the global supply chain and maintains the U.S. Strategic Materials Stockpile, which houses forty-two strategic commodities such as platinum, iridium, cobalt, and chromium, among others.

DSL (THE PRC DATA SECURITY LAW) Effective as of September 2021, this law covers data usage, collection, and protection, and it contains penalties for noncompliance.

EARs (EXPORT ADMINISTRATION REGULATIONS) Administered by the U.S. Department of Commerce, EARs regulate the export from the United States of "dual use" items, i.e., items with both commercial and military uses.

EAST INDIA COMPANY Founded in 1600, dissolved in 1874, it was a joint stock company as well as a form of nation-state that focused on trade in India, East Asia, and China. It was largely responsible for exploiting China through any and all means, including the sale of opium to the Chinese, which led to the first Opium War (1839–1842).

EBITDA (EARNINGS BEFORE INTEREST, TAXES, DEPRECIATION, AND AMORTIZATION) EBITDA is an accounting term used to calculate a company's profitability (earnings) before interest, taxes, depreciation, and amortization.

EEZs (EXCLUSIVE ECONOMIC ZONES, AS PRESCRIBED BY THE 1982 UNITED NATIONS CONVENTION ON THE LAW OF THE SEA) EEZs are areas extending no more than two hundred nautical miles beyond a country's coastlines in which a sovereign state has specialized rights, such as energy exploration.

EVERGRANDE A major Chinese private real estate developer that initially defaulted on loans in 2021 and filed for bankruptcy protection in the United States, Cayman Islands, and Hong Kong SAR in 2023.

EXON-FLORIO (THE EXON-FLORIO ACT OF 1988) Exon-Florio is a law that focuses on the national security implications of foreign direct investment in the United States.

FDI (FOREIGN DIRECT INVESTMENT) Refers to a business or real estate investment in one country by an individual or legal entity in another country.

FINSA (FOREIGN INVESTMENT AND NATIONAL SECURITY ACT) Enacted in July 2007, FINSA established a procedure for a U.S. governmental review (CFIUS) of certain foreign acquisitions targeting U.S. assets that may have national security implications.

FIRRMA (FOREIGN INVESTMENT RISK REVIEW MODERNIZATION ACT OF 2018) A law passed in 2018 that strengthens the procedures to evaluate foreign investments in the United States from the standpoint of national security.

FTZ (FOREIGN TRADE ZONE) A secure physical area considered outside those areas regulated by U.S. customs and border officials where foreign goods may be temporarily stored or handled.

GATT (GENERAL AGREEMENT ON TARIFFS AND TRADE) An international agreement originally signed in 1947 intended to promote international trade by reducing trade barriers. GATT was replaced by the World Trade Organization.

GDP (GROSS DOMESTIC PRODUCT) A country's GDP measures the monetary value of the goods and services it produces during a specific time period.

GREAT CHINESE FAMINE Ranked as one of the worst famines in history (1959–1961) when tens of millions of Chinese people are estimated to have died of starvation as a result of the Great Leap Forward.

GREAT LEAP FORWARD A failed social experiment by Mao Zedong from around 1958 to 1962, the Great Leap Forward sought to restructure China's population by setting up large rural communes sometimes staffed with forced labor, and resulting in the starvation of millions of Chinese.

GREY ZONE CONFLICT Refers to time periods between declared wars and peace when countries and nonstate groups engage in varying levels of competition to influence or threaten one another.

GUANXI A term that reflects an aspect of Chinese culture involving an individual's network of business and personal relationships and how they interact.

HKIAC (Hong Kong International Arbitration Centre) A nonprofit organization located in Hong Kong SAR that is a highly respected tribunal for resolving international commercial disputes.

Hu Jintao The leader of the People's Republic of China from 2002 to 2012; preceded Xi Jinping.

IATA (International Air Transport Association) A trade association composed of the world's major airlines located in Montreal, Quebec, Canada. The IATA exercises great influence over global air traffic rules and regulations.

ICAO (International Civil Aviation Organization) The ICAO is a specialized United Nations agency that focuses on safety in international air transport.

ICSID (International Centre for Settlement of Investment Disputes) A division of the World Bank Group.

ICT (information and communication technology) ICT refers to the infrastructure and physical devices that enable modern computing.

IFAD (International Fund for Agricultural Development) The IFAD is a United Nations specialized agency and financial institution with a mission to eradicate hunger and poor living conditions in developing countries.

IFC (International Finance Corporation) A division of the World Bank Group.

ILO (International Labor Organization) A United Nations specialized agency that works to create and enforce international labor standards.

IMF (INTERNATIONAL MONETARY FUND) An international organization with 190 member countries that promotes and implements economic policies in order to foster monetary cooperation and financial stability.

IMO (INTERNATIONAL MARITIME ORGANIZATION) A United Nations specialized agency, the IMO promotes safety and security regimes in international shipping and works to prevent pollution (air and water) by ships.

INTERNATIONAL BANK FOR RECONSTRUCTION AND DEVELOPMENT The lending-arm division of the World Bank Group.

INTERNATIONAL DEVELOPMENT ASSOCIATION A division of the World Bank Group that makes loans and grants to the poorest countries in the world.

IOC (INTERNATIONAL OLYMPIC COMMITTEE) A nongovernmental organization based in Lausanne, Switzerland; privately funded and organizes, among other events, the Summer and Winter Olympic Games.

IoT (INTERNET OF THINGS) IoT is the term that describes a complex and encompassing technology. It is a process by which massive amounts of digital data are captured from a potentially infinite number of sensors attached to individuals, machines, and other animate and inanimate objects connected to the internet. Once captured, the data can be used to direct a computer to handle an activity.

IP (INTELLECTUAL PROPERTY) IP includes written, musical, or artistic works, designs and symbols, names and images. IP inventions or creations can be protected by patents, copyrights, trademarks, and trade secrets.

IRC (INTERNATIONAL RESCUE COMMITTEE) The IRC is a nongovernmental organization that provides emergency aid and relief to those displaced by war, natural disaster, or persecution.

ISO (International Organization for Standardization)
The ISO is a nongovernmental, independent international entity that develops and sets standards intended to promote the safety, quality, and efficiency of products, services, and systems.

Just-in-time A management philosophy widely adopted in global markets by which a company tries to align the inflow of components and/or raw materials to the shortest possible time period so as to minimize inventory costs and still meet timely customer demands. It depends heavily on an efficient and uninterrupted supply chain.

Law of the Sea Treaty An international agreement that acts as the premier legal structure to oversee international maritime activities among the European Union and more than 165 member parties.

League of Nations Founded in 1920, the League of Nations was the world's first intergovernmental organization with the goal of achieving world peace.

Made in China 2025 China's national strategic plan adopted in 2015 to promote its manufacturing capabilities and achieve technological self-sufficiency by the year 2025.

Mao Zedong A controversial figure who was at first a revolutionary and then served as chair of the Chinese Communist Party from 1949 until his death in 1976.

Marshall Plan Enacted by the U.S. Congress in 1948, the Marshall Plan was a massive foreign aid package that targeted economic recovery for the countries of Western Europe that were devastated following World War II.

MaxTrend®/MaxTrends® A development or event that has the potential to impact a country, business, or individual, positively or negatively, in such a way as to affect their policies or goals.

MOFCOM (**China's Ministry of Commerce**) An executive-level agency in China charged with formulating policies on foreign trade, exports and imports, foreign direct investment, and negotiation strategies (multilateral and bilateral) on behalf of China.

NAFTA (**North American Free Trade Agreement**) An international treaty implemented in 1994 between Mexico, Canada, and the United States, it eliminated or reduced tariffs on most goods and services traded between the three nations in a large free trade zone. NAFTA was replaced in September 2018 by the United States-Mexico-Canada Agreement (USMCA).

Nation-state A sovereign government that rules over a defined geographic territory. Nation-states control borders, manage currencies, and enforce laws. In theory, each nation-state is made up of a homogenous population sharing common goals and a common culture.

National Security Law (Law of the People's Republic of China on Safeguarding National Security in the Hong Kong Special Administrative Region) Enacted in June 2020, this law criminalizes a large range of activities for Hong Kong residents and others who are not permanent residents of Hong Kong.

NATO (**the North Atlantic Treaty Organization**) An intergovernmental military alliance with thirty-one member states that enforces the North Atlantic Treaty (1949).

NCSC (**National Counterintelligence and Security Center**) Acts to counter serious threats to U.S. assets and information for both the U.S. government and private sector players.

NDRC (**China's National Development and Reform Commission**) A ministerial-level department of the state council that oversees policies and decisions on development and reform and implements strategies of medium- and long-term plans.

New Development Bank (formerly BRICS Development Bank) A multinational development bank established by the BRICS group of countries (Brazil, Russia, India, China, and South Africa).

New York Convention (the UN Convention on the Recognition and Enforcement of Foreign Arbitral Awards) The global agreement that permits the transfer and enforcement of arbitral awards among member states.

NIST (National Institute for Standards and Technology) Performs a number of functions, including providing services for creating measurements and standards for U.S. industries, federal agencies, and the general public, including cybersecurity.

One-child policy A strictly enforced government policy in China from 1979 through 2015 intended to limit population growth.

Opium Wars A series of battles fought between the Qing Dynasty and the British Empire. The Chinese were attempting to suppress the British who were illegally smuggling opium into China in an attempt to open up China to more trade.

Paris Accord (aka Paris Agreement) The binding international treaty adopted in 2015 that deals with efforts to mitigate climate change by reducing gases that are contributing to global warming and its effects.

PEPFAR (President's Emergency Plan for AIDS Relief) A U.S.-funded program designed to counteract HIV/AIDS in Africa; over the last twenty years PEPFAR has provided over $100 billion in relief.

PLA (People's Liberation Army) The principal military force of the People's Republic of China, composed of the Ground Force, Air Force, Navy, Strategic Support Force, and the Rocket Force.

PLAN (People's Liberation Army Navy) The maritime service branch of the People's Liberation Army.

QUAD The Quadrilateral Security Dialogue is a diplomatic relationship between four countries—India, Australia, Japan, and the United States—that attempts to promote a free and open Indo-Pacific region.

RCEP (REGIONAL COMPREHENSIVE ECONOMIC PARTNERSHIP) A regional free trade agreement composed of Australia, China, Japan, Republic of Korea, and New Zealand as well as the ASEAN countries (Brunei, Cambodia, Indonesia, Laos, Malaysia, Myanmar, the Philippines, Singapore, Thailand, and Vietnam). The RCEP's focus is to promote an open multilateral trading network.

REEs (RARE EARTH ELEMENTS) Valuable mineral materials that must be extracted from refined ores. REEs are in high demand by many technologically oriented industries.

RMB (RENMINBI) The official currency of China is denoted as either the renminbi (RMB) or the yuan (CYN). Technically, the renminbi acts as the actual medium of exchange. The yuan is the unit of account used by China's government within the Chinese financial system.

SCRM (SUPPLY CHAIN RISK MANAGEMENT) A methodology that is intended to first assess supply chain risks and then address mitigation of those risks.

SEZs (SPECIAL ECONOMIC ZONES) SEZs exist in a number of countries around the world. Chinese SEZs are those defined areas that operate under free-market-oriented economic policies that are intended to attract foreign direct investment.

SHADOW BANKS Banking entities in China; sometimes called trust companies, they provide high-interest loans and financing outside the traditional banking sector and so are largely unregulated.

SHERMAN ANTITRUST ACT OF 1890 Attempted to rein in the power and influence of America's largest corporations in the early 20th century.

SIPRI (Stockholm International Peace Research Institute)
An international research institute founded in Stockholm, Sweden, in 1966; provides analysis and recommendations about the arms trade, military expenditures, and arms control.

SOEs (state-owned enterprises) More than half of China's market capitalization is dominated by state-owned enterprises. It is estimated that there are more than 150,000 Chinese SOEs. China's economy depends heavily on the contributions of SOEs, though many are viewed as inefficient and underperforming.

Taizong Second emperor of the Tang Dynasty who ruled China from 626 CE to 649 CE; considered one of the most enlightened emperors in China's history.

Tang Dynasty Considered the "golden age" of Chinese history, the Tang Dynasty reigned between 618 CE and 907 CE (except for a brief interregnum between 690 CE and 705 CE). Scholars and historians believe that it was a prolific period for the arts, and that great advances were made during this time in China's educational system, religious practices, and social networks.

TPP (Trans-Pacific Partnership) The TPP was initially a proposed trade agreement between twelve countries in the Pacific region. Shortly after taking office in 2017, President Trump withdrew U.S. participation.

TRA (Taiwan Relations Act) The original act was passed in 1979 and promoted the security interests and stability of Taiwan by the United States, unofficially acknowledging a nondiplomatic relationship with Taiwan while still officially recognizing the People's Republic of China.

Treaty of Nanking This treaty was signed in 1842 following China's defeat in the First Opium War and led to the 150-year lease of Hong Kong Island to the British and the broad grant of trading rights in China to Western powers.

UEL (Unreliable Entity List) The UEL is a mechanism administered by MOFCOM that identifies specific foreign (non-Chinese) individuals or entities that have cut off supplies to Chinese companies for noncommercial purposes. Identified entities or individuals may be prohibited from engaging in investment and/or import–export activities with China.

UNCLOS (United Nations Convention on the Law of the Sea) An international treaty that attempts to establish and enforce a legal framework for all maritime activities.

UNCTAD (United Nations Conference on Trade and Development) UNCTAD was created to resolve investment, trade, and development issues and is a part of the United Nations Secretariat. UNCTAD helps developing countries accelerate their economic development by fostering trade opportunities and projects with more developed countries.

UNDP (United Nations Development Programme; includes the UNCDF [UN Capital Development Fund] and the UNV [United Nations Volunteers]) The UNDP focuses on addressing the needs of the world's most vulnerable individuals and regions.

UNEP (United Nations Environment Programme) The UNEP focuses its efforts on global environmental issues.

UNESCO (United Nations Educational, Scientific and Cultural Organization) An agency operating under the umbrella of the United Nations that promotes international cooperation in education, arts, sciences, and culture.

UNHCR (Office of the United Nations High Commissioner for Refugees) The UNHCR focuses on the needs of refugees and displaced individuals and communities.

USMCA (United States-Mexico-Canada Agreement) The USMCA is an international trade agreement that replaced NAFTA on July 1, 2020. According to the U.S. Trade Representative, the USMCA was designed to support "North American manufacturing and mutually beneficial trade."

WHO (World Health Organization) The WHO is a specialized agency of the United Nations focusing on international health issues and concerns.

World Bank Group An international organization with 189 countries as members, the World Bank is the largest funding source for underwriting investments relating to climate change and economic development. It has five institutions: the International Bank for Reconstruction and Development; the International Development Association; the International Finance Corporation; the Multilateral Investment Guarantee Agency; and the International Centre for Settlement of Investment Disputes.

WTO (World Trade Organization) The WTO is an international UN organization that establishes rules of trade between countries with the goal of facilitating trade flows with as few barriers as possible.

Xi Jinping Current leader of the People's Republic of China; succeeded Hu Jintao in 2013.

Xi Zhongxun Father of Xi Jinping and a veteran CCP member who fought alongside Mao prior to 1949; demoted and reportedly jailed by Mao during the Cultural Revolution.

Yuan The official currency of China is denoted as either the renminbi (RMB) or the yuan (CYN). Technically, the renminbi acts as the actual medium of exchange. The yuan is the unit of account used by China's government within the Chinese financial system.

YUAN DYNASTY (1271 CE TO 1368 CE) The Yuan Dynasty was composed of tribes of Mongolian ancestry that replaced the Song Dynasty, which had ruled China for almost three centuries. Kublai Khan was the first Yuan emperor and unified China.

ZERO-COVID (OR COVID-ZERO) POLICY A failed attempt to prevent the spread of COVID-19 in China which led to lockdowns and maximum suppression resulting in severe economic consequences.

ZHU DI Third emperor of the Ming Dynasty, he attempted to expand China's influence around the world; his son Zhu Gaosui abandoned his father's dream and forced China into self-imposed isolation.

ZHU GAOSUI Son of Emperor Zhu Di; upon his father's death forced China into self-imposed isolation that lasted for nearly 500 years until the early 20th century.

ACKNOWLEDGMENTS

No author should ever try to take all of the credit for writing a book. I don't. Every book is a collaborative process. I owe a deep debt of gratitude to Kimberly McSparran, my talented executive assistant for over thirty years; Diane Braun for her valuable research skills; Bruce Wexler for his expert advice in shaping this book; David Hornik for his skillful copyediting; Beth Ansell for inspiring the cover art; and John Palmer, who taught me to be a better writer. Then there are the many uncredited individuals who have shared with me their own experiences, insights, and stories that appear throughout the book. I am grateful to each of you. Finally, my thanks to Roger Kimball and Elizabeth Bachmann of Encounter Books for publishing this book. My hope is that readers will find learning more about Xi Jinping and China as interesting as I do.

—Dennis Unkovic

NOTES

CHAPTER ONE

1 Xi Zhongxun was eventually "rehabilitated" in 1975, shortly before Mao's death.

CHAPTER TWO

1 This was ironic, since it was Marco Polo who had initially sparked Chinese expansionism while at the same time making the Europeans aware of the unique products and riches available in the Far East.

CHAPTER THREE

1 MaxTrend® and MaxTrends® are registered trademarks in the United States and in many countries around the world.

2 The Belt and Road Initiative began in 2013 and is the largest infrastructure project in the history of the world. Its goal is to link sixty countries in Asia, Africa, and Europe by constructing a series of roads, ports, railroads, and airports so those countries are permanently tied to China as their primary source for manufactured goods and components.

CHAPTER FOUR

1 Demographers study population densities by analyzing births, deaths, and aging, and then make predictions on how those trends will impact—for better or worse—a nation's economic growth prospects.

2 This is not just a Chinese phenomenon; birth rates everywhere around the world tend to drop as financial security is achieved.

CHAPTER SIX

1 There are fifty REEs included on the *2022 Final List of Critical Minerals* as defined in the U.S. Geological Survey (which is part of the U.S. Department of the Interior): Aluminum, antimony, arsenic, barite, beryllium, bismuth, cerium, cesium, chromium, cobalt, dysprosium, erbium, europium, fluorspar, gadolinium, gallium, germanium, graphite, hafnium, holmium, indium, iridium, lanthanum, lithium, lutetium, magnesium, manganese, neodymium, nickel, niobium, palladium, platinum, praseodymium, rhodium, rubidium, ruthenium, samarium, scandium, tantalum, tellurium, terbium, thulium, tin, titanium, tungsten, vanadium, ytterbium, yttrium, zinc, and zirconium.

2 The balance of REE reserves are located in Australia, Brazil, the United States, Malaysia, India, Russia, and a handful of other countries.

3 China and Japan have fought over ownership of the Senkaku Islands for decades.

CHAPTER SEVEN

1 China in 2024 will be lucky to grow at 4 percent.

CHAPTER EIGHT

1 As China began to develop as a manufacturing center in the 1980s, new jobs were created in special economic zones, many of which were located along the Pacific coast of China from Shenzhen in the south as far as Tianjin and Harbin in the north. As these SEZs grew, significant numbers of younger workers willingly relocated from rural areas of China to work in those factories where they could earn much higher salaries. Millions of Chinese work along the coast in industrial parks.

CHAPTER NINE

1 According to sources, the world's ten most industrialized countries in 2023 were China, the United States, Japan, Germany, India, South Korea, the United Kingdom, France, Italy, and Mexico.

CHAPTER TEN

1 Water pollution is not a China-only problem. Although over two-thirds of the earth is covered with water, less than 3 percent of that water is considered potable (meaning it can be safely consumed without first being significantly treated with chemicals). Today the major world cities of Beijing, Cairo, Jakarta, Moscow, Istanbul, London, Tokyo, Mexico City, Miami, Sao Paulo, and Bangalore are all experiencing increasingly critical potable-water shortages.

2 As described elsewhere in this book, China's Belt and Road Initiative is one policy being promoted actively today. One part of this initiative is the creation of dams along the Mekong River.

CHAPTER TWELVE

1 A "blue-water" strategy for a naval power means the ability of a navy to project itself not just in coastal regions but throughout larger parts of the world. The world's leading naval power is the U.S. Navy, which can project itself anywhere in either a defensive or an offensive posture. It is a true blue-water navy.

2 Declassified in 1992, the bunker is now open to public tours.

3 The nine-dash line encompasses approximately 90 percent of the South China Sea. China claims sole sovereignty within this area.

4 The Spratly Islands are made up of more than one hundred mostly small islands and reefs. China, Taiwan, and Vietnam claim sovereignty over the archipelago, and some parts are claimed by the Philippines and Malaysia.

5 The Malacca Straits have historically been a vital shipping lane for global trade going both east and west.

6 It should be noted that military service in South Korea is not mandatory for women, although women are permitted to enlist.

CHAPTER THIRTEEN

1 Curiously around this same time, China began a hard push to be admitted to the World Trade Organization (WTO) and finally succeeded in December 2001. Clearly China was embracing multilateral organizations and free trade as a way to promote its economy.

2 For a more detailed explanation of CFIUS, see Appendix 1.

3 There are similarities in how different countries attempt to restrict outside investors that do not align with their interests. The first set of criteria a country uses when determining whether to flag an FDI transaction is called a "threshold." A threshold is a certain percentage of voting rights or assets of the domestic entity that is being targeted by a foreign investor. Each country is free to set its own thresholds, though in some instances international governing bodies can be involved. When a transaction anticipates that the percentage of the assets and rights transferred is higher than the threshold, the transaction will require formal screening. Furthermore, there are some sectors where, regardless of the threshold, a government will decide the transaction must come under review. News-media outlets and aviation are examples of such sectors.

4 Appendix 2 contains a discussion of how the United Kingdom, Germany, France, Italy, Spain, the Netherlands, Japan, and Canada are cracking down on foreign direct investment.

CHAPTER FOURTEEN

1 Excluding the drug and pharmaceutical industry, which is a world unto itself.

2 Made in China 2025 was a strategic plan instituted in 2013 to decrease China's dependence on foreign technologies and instead to develop Chinese-based technologies.

CHAPTER SIXTEEN

1 When the U.S. Senate is in session, which is when bills are introduced and debated, rarely are all or even most of the one hundred senators present; they are often absent for a variety of reasons until the actual vote is taken.

2 An in-depth explanation of the four basic intellectual property protection vehicles—patents, trademarks, copyrights, and trade secrets—can be found in Appendix 5.

3 Perhaps the best example of a trade secret is the formula for Coca-Cola®. The creators of the formula in the late 1800s realized that a patent on the formula would only last for twenty years, after which the recipe would become publicly available. The company's owner, Dr. John S. Pemberton, instead opted to keep the formula as a trade secret, and as such the formula has never been disclosed. Apparently only two company employees at any given time know the formula.

CHAPTER SEVENTEEN

1 Other disputes over the South China Sea also arose. During the 1990s, Vietnam and China waged ongoing arguments over portions of the South China Sea located closest to Vietnam. Even the United States became embroiled in the controversy in 2009, when five Chinese ships harassed a U.S. ocean surveillance vessel while it was in international waters in the South China Sea.

2 Hillary Clinton, Donald Trump's Democratic opponent in the 2016 presidential campaign, also questioned the advisability for the United States to remain an active member of the TPP.

3 Because of the potential impact on countries bordering the South China Sea, ironically one of the big winners might be India because of its proximity to Europe and North America.

CHAPTER EIGHTEEN

1 "Informatization" or "informatisation" is defined as the extent to which a geographic area, economy, or society is becoming information-based.

CHAPTER NINETEEN

1 If an economy grows at 8 percent, it will double every eight and a half years. China managed to do this again and again.

2 Because of COVID-19 protocols, the drone presentation was actually produced in Shenzhen and broadcast at the time of the Olympics, but still this drone technology was some of the most advanced in the world.

3 Interestingly, Israel, much like the United States, has focused on R&D funding for the military and leading academic centers as well as creating joint ventures.

CHAPTER TWENTY

1 Many, including African leaders themselves, had expected Africa to receive more attention and focus than it did from President Barack Obama.

2 The PEPFAR program was directed in part by Dr. Anthony Fauci, who became well known to most of the general public during the COVID-19 pandemic.

CHAPTER TWENTY-ONE

1 The WTO sets global rules of trade that it expects its members to follow. In exchange, members of the WTO face lower trade barriers and are able to carry out activities with other WTO member countries that would not be possible otherwise.

2 The Clinton Administration also hoped that bringing China into the WTO would over time lead to a more democratized China. Obviously this did not come to pass.

CHAPTER TWENTY-TWO

1 Numerous individuals over the years have questioned whether this wonderful quote truly comes from Mark Twain. No one knows for sure.

CHAPTER TWENTY-THREE

1 In a sense, Hong Kong is a microcosm of greater China. Hong Kong is proof of how an autocratic system can mightily impose its will on a society. In 1997, China promised fifty years of independence to Hong Kong. It broke that promise. As an epilogue, I wrote a personal memoir and titled it "Good Night, Hong Kong."

APPENDIX 1

1 TID stands for "technology, infrastructure, and data."

APPENDIX 3

1 If you would like to know more about Professor Ang's analysis, I recommend her 2020 book *China's Gilded Age: The Paradox of Economic Boom and Vast Corruption*.

APPENDIX 5

1 This "freedom," however, does not extend to exportation of the product back to the United States or to any other country where patent protection has been granted.

APPENDIX 6

1 These figures do not include Hong Kong SAR, Macao SAR, and Taiwan.

INDEX